FORTRESS AMERICA

FORTRESS AMERICA

THE AMERICAN MILITARY AND THE CONSEQUENCES OF PEACE

-◄O►-

WILLIAM GREIDER

PUBLICAFFAIRS

New York

Book design by Jenny Dossin.

LIBRARY OF CONGRESS CATALOGING-IN-PUBLICATION DATA

GREIDER, WILLIAM.

FORTRESS AMERICA : THE AMERICAN MILITARY AND THE
CONSEQUENCES OF PEACE / WILLIAM GREIDER.

P.   CM.

ISBN 1-891620-45-2

1. ECONOMIC CONVERSION—UNITED STATES.

2. DISARMAMENT—ECONOMIC ASPECTS—UNITED STATES.

3. UNITED STATES—DEFENSES—ECONOMIC ASPECTS.

4. MILITARY-INDUSTRIAL COMPLEX—UNITED STATES.   I. TITLE.

HC110.D4G74   1998

330.973'0929—DC21

98-30426

CIP

1 3 5 7 9 10 8 6 4 2

CONTENTS

FORTRESS AMERICA

WHEN THE GREAT WAR ENDED, AMERICANS HELD NO HOMECOMING PARADES TO COMMEMORATE THE HISTORIC VICTORY. IN A SENSE, THERE WAS NO need because celebrations were playing out elsewhere in the world, again and again, in the form of spontaneous pageants.

Joyous young people climbing atop the Berlin Wall, dismantling it brick by brick. Citizens in Eastern Europe surging across national borders that had been closed for two generations. Soviet icons toppled in the town squares of Poland and Lithuania, even Russia. Lenin's bust smashed to rubble, Stalin's alongside it. Then the Soviet Union itself dissolved, a long-lived demon cast into oblivion.

So the Cold War ended. Peace was resumed. New governments were formed, new constitutions adopted, and dozens of satellite republics became autonomous nations again. The rush of commerce and finance, east and west, ratified the new political reality as a huge segment of the world's population reentered the fluid tides of trade and investment that had been blocked for roughly forty-five years. Although the process of economic reunification produced social upheavals, occasional reversals, and many disappointments, it had begun with furious energy and hope.

That was only ten years ago, but given the manic pace at which we now live, it seems like ages. One large reality has not changed, however: the United States remains mobilized for world war, or perhaps to fight many smaller wars at once, wherever they might arise. Meanwhile, we stand guard over global peace, perhaps defend it whenever it may be threatened.

This is not just remarkable; it is unprecedented. When the Cold War ended, America did not demobilize, as it had after previous great conflicts. True, the awesome U.S. military arsenal was reduced in size, but it remains configured and equipped to confront a war of maximum scale, prompted by some large and unknowable threat that no one can yet name.

The defense budget was reduced significantly, but only to a level around $260 billion. Adjusted for inflation, that is about what the United States was spending to counter the Soviet Union twenty years ago, when Jimmy Carter was president and Cold War tensions were heightened.

The vast industrial structure required to support and supply the armed forces underwent its own shrinkage and consolidation but also continues in place with massive capabilities, still inventing and producing, still imagining a next generation of advanced weaponry that can prevail over this unnamed future enemy.

Congress, two presidents, the public at large, and both political parties have all seemed to find nothing strange in this. America remains expensively ready for war. No one in authority dares question this, and the public does not ask: to what end?

This book, intended as a sympathetic wake-up call, is designed to provoke a much livelier discussion of big questions nearly everyone now wishes to avoid. What exactly is the purpose of Fortress America now that our only serious adversary has evaporated into history? What are the real costs of imagining new foreign dangers simply to sustain the status quo? Above all, can the nation really afford the price of its own inertia?

Since no one can know what the future will throw at us, I do not pretend that these or other questions are to be neatly resolved here. This is not going to be another what-if catalog of potential enemies around the globe or a geopolitical explanation of why another big war seems most unlikely. I'm not going to analyze the defense budget and force structure, sector by sector, looking for obvious excess. Nor am I setting out to make sophisticated comparisons of the competing weapons systems—which ones seem promising and which might be discarded. I do not choose sides in the perennial rivalries between the Navy, the Air Force, and the Army. I do not make a case for either fearing or embracing China, not to mention the various "rogue" nations regularly nominated as the next big test of American resolve.

This book instead assembles evidence for a single proposition that underlies all other questions: the U.S. military-industrial complex, as we have known it, is in the process of devouring itself, literally and tangibly. The awesome interlocking structure of armed forces, industrial interests, and political alliances that has sprawled across American public life and purpose for two generations cannot endure for long, not in its familiar shape and size.

This is not a matter of political choices or foreign threats. It is the hard, unacknowledged consequence of peace. The existing defense institution is too large to sustain, too backward-looking in design, too ambitious in its preparations for future war. Yet it is also too settled and powerful to think of undertaking fundamental change. So it feeds on itself. Why? Because, unable or unwilling to change, the defense establishment is compelled, by the general peace, to sustain itself by steadily sacrificing vital parts of itself.

A central purpose of this book is to make visible the profound paradox that confronts the military institution: U.S. forces are, without question, the best and most powerful in the world, and yet they also are steadily, strangely becoming dysfunctional. Fortress America is overwhelmed by peace because it is still trying to meet the obligations of the old, full-scale mobilization.

The military is committed to maintaining a gigantic scale and structure inherited from the Cold War, but with reduced resources for the workaday tasks of training people and maintaining an active state of readiness.

The Pentagon and defense industry are likewise committed to producing the next generation of more advanced weapons, which were originally conceived during the Cold War. Yet that commitment imposes even more demanding challenges for training the men and women who must learn to operate the new war-making technology. Moreover, the military expects somehow to buy these new planes, ships, and missiles on its reduced procurement budgets.

Meanwhile, military thinkers are sketching out more distant plans and concepts for a futuristic warfare conducted by fantastic new methods and systems. They intend to invent and build this future war-fighting capability while they keep paying for everything else—all the present forces and new weapons already in the pipeline.

It does not add up. Quite literally, there is no way to pay for all these competing claims. So defense leaders hack away at what they can—cutting this and that from present forces, from weapons purchases, from training and other basic necessities, robbing one account to keep another account temporarily solvent. That process steadily weakens the various parts of the defense apparatus in order to maintain the appearance that nothing has changed. The impact is debilitating and essentially incoherent, since it is based on no plausible logic for the future other than wishful thinking.

America could decide, of course, to reverse direction and begin pumping up its defense budgets again. (That's what some military sectors yearn for.) This turn of events appears most unlikely, however, for various political and fiscal reasons. It also begs the question of purpose: to what end? If the world is at peace, why should America now have to remobilize? There are no persuasive answers at present.

To justify the significant budget increases that might rescue the military from its dilemma of competing obligations, political leaders will first have to find convincing dangers—a rising threat of actual war, and on a very large scale. Until they can do so, military leaders must keep hacking away at their own institution.

People in the armed services know this. They can see it happening. One large irony of the present national predicament is that politicians and citizens may avert their gaze but the threatening situation is inescapable and visible every day for men and women in uniform. They feel the squeeze in numerous ways and experience the gloom and confusion of having suddenly lost the great purpose in what they are expected to do. We will see their human and professional tensions up close, through their eyes, as we visit some military bases of all three services.

The dilemma is also familiar to the men and women who work in the factories that make the aircraft, tanks, ships, missiles, and munitions. More than one million of them have lost their jobs during the last decade. But their employers, the defense manufacturers, have managed to solve a great riddle of business enterprise: how to prosper in a shrinking market. We will unravel that riddle as we tour the defense industry from the factory floor to corporate headquarters to the stock market.

The dramatic consolidation of defense companies has left an impression that at least the industrial side of the military-industrial complex has been rationally restructured. That belief is wildly mistaken, as we shall see. Despite a dramatic downsizing in employment, the structure of the defense industry remains enormously bloated with overcapacity—too many factories, with not enough sales to keep the factories busy. The government pays for this surplus of productive capacity.

The industry, like the services, seems poised for an unlikely rejuvenation, clinging to the frail expectation that somehow or other defense spending can be made to surge again. This is a very costly wish, but the cost is borne by others, namely, the taxpayers.

Finally, as smart warriors are expected to do in peacetime, various military leaders try to imagine what the next war will look like and to prepare for it. Whether their vision is accurate or fanciful, the new thinking is blocked by the status quo, which, embedded in people's minds by the long contest with the Soviet superpower, prevents the imagining of anything but a surprisingly similar (though unidentified) adversary for the future. The reflexive appetite for repeating the successful past also stands in the way of pursuing different strategic assumptions.

As this suggests, the basic methodologies of war-planning and execution inherited from the Cold War decades are still very much in place, still defining both the armed services and the arms industry. These are deeply held habits of thought. As we make our tour of various military landscapes, we will begin to appreciate how difficult it is for the military and industry to abandon them in the absence of concerted political pressures to do so.

One of the Cold War's enduring premises is massive redundancy—that is, staggering numbers of accumulated weapons (and warriors) meant to intimidate potential enemies and positioned to prevail in a long conflict if necessary. When the U.S.

objective was preparing to wage a broad-front war in Central Europe, the awesome surpluses of backup firepower could perhaps be justified (that is, if one believed the plausibility of a Soviet invasion of Germany). But what exactly is the point of storing and maintaining the same sort of overkill in Texas?

The desire for deep redundancy in firepower collides, as it always did, with another imperative from the Cold War: the endless search for invention. The military and industry remain united in their desire to invent and produce new generations of high-tech weapons systems that will trump superior numbers of less sophisticated armaments fielded by a less advanced industrial society. That costly search continues now, but without the Soviet adversary present to justify it. Indeed, the brilliant *new* weapons systems to be produced by the United States seem most threatening to the already brilliant *existing* weapons systems in the U.S. arsenal, since those are themselves without peer anywhere in the world.

The political base that always supported the Cold War defense structure endures, too, without a strategy for the future except to change as little as possible from the past. It is easy enough to blame the lack of new direction and serious policy debate on the politicians, but that misses the larger point: the public doesn't wish to face these questions either.

After decades of living with the Soviet threat, people are naturally not eager to hear about new dangers, real or imaginary. Without a convincing specter of nuclear Armageddon, citizens (and the news media) drift off to other, less frightening subjects. We *are* at peace, after all. Not surprisingly, Americans want to talk about something else and would just as soon not think about the subject of war-making.

In other words, as a society, America has still not absorbed the implications of its triumph. Now that it is over, we are only beginning to appreciate how profoundly the Cold War organized our public life after World War II, even our way of thinking about ourselves as a nation. It provided the central purpose for the country, the imperative that preempted all issues. It gave us a righteous sense of ourselves as actors in the world, pursuing large principles on behalf of others as well as our national security. Cold War events also provided us, to be blunt, with a sense of thrill and adventure—a dramatic narrative of good guys battling against the bad guys on many fronts. The story line permeated not just our politics but our popular culture.

The unifying purpose also conveniently masked the standard ideological arguments about the role of government in private economic sectors. Conservatives who might resist federal regulation of business or economic pump-priming had no difficulty whatever supporting the government as the sole investor in, buyer for, and manager of the vast industrial complex required for the Cold War. Left-liberal critics might take occasional pokes at these contradictions in "military socialism," but, of course, they also wanted the job creation and economic growth that flowed from defense spending.

So did the universities and research centers, the engineers and scientists who cooperated in and prospered from the permanent mobilization of technology the Cold War required. So did organized labor and thousands of communities: in both arenas it was recognized that defense jobs and military bases delivered economic development of high quality and permanence.

At every level of society, institutions of every kind accepted and adapted to the imperatives of the Cold War struggle. The complex politics that grew up around the defense budget, including its wasteful and corrupting aspects, has been examined and reexamined. The process has resembled a sophisticated form of log-rolling—mutual trading and back-scratching among states and companies and service branches. Everyone learned how to play and how to benefit.

The three armed services, dependent upon congressional support for every aspect of their well-being, dispersed their installations accordingly and sponsored design competitions for new weapons that would keep weaker companies alive with the hope of winning the next round. Prime contractors likewise created their own far-flung geography of subcontractors and suppliers so they could demonstrate to wavering senators or representatives precisely how many good jobs and contracts were at stake back home. If a new bomber of dubious purpose was being rolled out for production, it helped that hundreds of congressional districts were building pieces of it.

xvi

Is that political game over? Not yet. As I'll show, it is premature to claim that the political community is ready to face up to the meaning of the end of the Cold War and to change long-held habits. Indeed, the specter of losing the reliable vigor of defense spending has probably intensified the political contest for dwindling assets. And while Congress accepted the closure of one hundred or so military bases, it has sullenly declared: no more. The truth is, though procurement spending fell sharply, the various political alliances refuse to give up on any of the military-industrial plans for the next round of fighter planes, ships, and missiles, despite the weakening rationales for them, and despite inadequate defense budgets.

My core argument is that the status quo in national defense is not going to survive these internal contradictions—the conflicting ambitions and obligations, the steady erosion of superb defense capabilities, the confusion of sustaining outmoded purposes. Whether or not these matters are faced directly in a vigorous national debate, the military-industrial system, as we have known it, is bound to be steadily weakened—and to become even more incoherent—if it stays the present course. Juggling budget accounts has deferred and concealed the crisis, but its dimensions are already visible, as we shall see.

In some ways, the money is the least of it. The larger and more troubling political questions are about purpose. What is America becoming to the world as the sole surviving superpower? Does it intend to manage the global future as a sort of

xvii

noblesse-oblige imperium? Do Americans really want to maintain an empire? And if events should turn bloody and dangerous somewhere remote from U.S. national interest, will Americans support this abstract burden as reliably as they supported the Cold War struggle?

During the Cold War years, the idea of a permanent threat to ourselves and the virtuous campaign to liberate others from tyranny seemed, in some ways, a good fit with the national character and history, from the "manifest destiny" of westward conquest to our shared, sacred principles of freedom and democracy.

But did the Cold War change the American character in other ways? Public opinion suggests that, while Americans are not isolationist, they have an abiding and well-earned skepticism about engaging themselves in the distant fights of other peoples. Is this reluctance provincial immaturity or native wisdom? Is it still possible to imagine the country and national purpose that existed before there was a permanent mobilization for war, before open-ended and undefined global obligations existed?

We are going to find the answers to these questions, I fear, sooner or later. Even posing them may seem nostalgic to many, but they are back on the table again, unacknowledged, begging for a serious discussion. So long as they remain unaddressed, our country's inertia has us drifting toward a moment of unpleasant surprise—when things go wrong and questions of national purpose are fully debated again but in the most inflammatory circumstances.

xviii

In short, our tour of Fortress America is about more than defense spending in an era of general peace. It's about national vision and the limits of empire, about whether Americans really wish to govern the world with U.S. military power. Finally, I seek to stimulate discussion of the alternative possibilities—of a very different understanding of what might someday threaten us and how to maintain a stable world order that is not defined by superpower rivalry or by American empire.

Beyond the Cold War, global peacekeeping may rely more fundamentally on defending shared values and economic interests among very different peoples, rich and poor, across race, religion, culture, and history. This is a new world order that will require much more than the accumulation of weaponry, and it might even be subverted by a new global arms race.

America is positioned to lead the world toward a new system; right now, the nation is not even talking about these prospects.

For now, the issues of national defense seem more prosaic and concrete. The sprawling apparatus of armaments created to win the Cold War still exists, even if people have forgotten its size and complexity. The machines and troops are still busy every day maintaining their readiness for combat, while complacent Americans still pay for this expensive process. New, more capable fighter planes are going into production, while the very capable older models are sold to foreign buyers.

This is not an abstraction. You can see the problem every day in Fortress America.

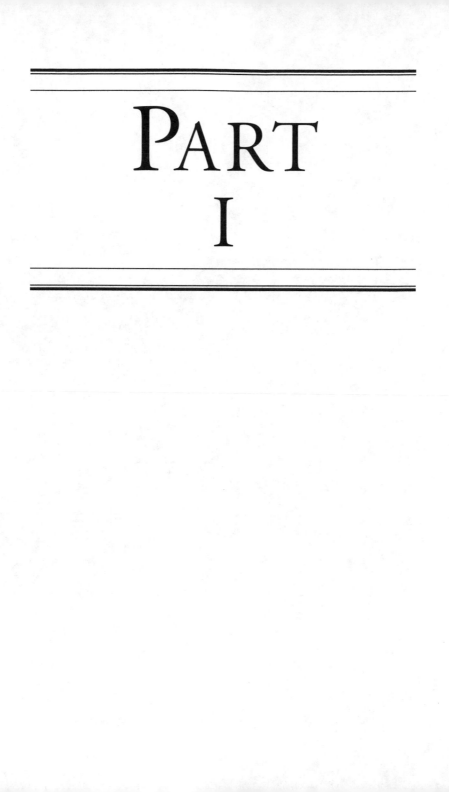

PART I

CHAPTER ONE

VIRTUAL TANKS

THE GUNS OF FORT HOOD ARE POINTING WESTWARD, LIKE A MIGHTY ARMY PARKED ON THE CENTRAL TEXAS PRAIRIE. ONE TURNS REFLEXIVELY TOWARD the horizon to see what all the tanks are aimed at. An attacking force from Abilene? Invasion by New Mexico? Nothing in sight. The land dies away in scrubby emptiness, miles of dimpled, treeless prairie save for occasional clusters of stubborn live oaks. Texas is at peace, like the rest of America, but still ready to fight.

The main post at Fort Hood looks bland and spartan, like any other Army base, but it is distinguished for its firepower. Forty percent of the U.S. Army's combat power is located here—two heavy divisions of tanks and mechanized infantry, the III Corps command, plus numerous supporting units. Some forty-three thousand people are stationed at Fort Hood, making it the largest installation in the armed services.

North of the main post, just beyond a low ridge, are the open ranges—nearly two hundred thousand acres of unpopulated prairie available for live-fire training, tank maneuvers, aerial attacks, and practice battles with ground-launched missiles, mortars, machine guns, and grenade launchers. One of the ranges is a small European village with narrow streets, close-together stores and houses. This place where tank commanders learn to maneuver in an urban environment is like a movie set with false facades.

Between payroll and contracts, the base generates about $2 billion a year in local economic activity; Lieutenant Colonel Randy School, chief of information, observes that "Fort Hood is, in effect, the largest corporation in the state of Texas."

Killeen, the small town next door, appears to be prospering and to have acquired every fast-food franchise known to man. Most of the soldiers, men and women, are married and live off-base with families in working-class subdivisions. Their neighborhoods look different from the rest of America only in that the people are thoroughly integrated by race, like the military itself. The kids walking home from school in late afternoon are a multicultural stream of white, black, Asian, Hispanic, and some attractive combinations. Some of them get picked up by moms or dads in fatigues.

Fort Hood may consume a lot of public money, but nobody gets rich serving in the armed forces. Like other military towns, Killeen has its seedy highway strip of tattoo parlors and Saturday night bust-out bars, interspersed with numerous pawn shops. Personal debt is a big problem for many soldiers. The post provides regular counseling on managing money.

"There are soldiers here on Fort Hood who are on food stamps," Colonel School informs me. "I had a soldier here in this office, married with three kids, who figured out that if he rejected his military subsistence allowance, he qualified for food stamps and he came out dollars ahead. He decided not to do it. Too proud."

4

Peace puts its own strange pressures on people in uniform, both from downsizing adjustments and the repetition of minor missions abroad. "I'll tell you: the Army is a stressful place these days," the colonel remarks. "This corps has about six thousand people deployed away from home—thirty-two hundred Fort Hood soldiers in Kuwait, sixteen hundred soldiers in Bosnia, then lots of smaller units around the world. And a lot of these soldiers have been over there multiple times. They're excited and positive about doing their job, but remember, this is a married Army, and that spouse back home is not keen on this. The spouse says: 'Honey, this is no way to live.'"

Another, perhaps more significant source of stress at Fort Hood involves machines, not people. The wondrous machinery of modern land warfare is assembled here in such gross abundance that it rises to the level of spectacle, an American marvel. The kind of attraction tourists might bring the kids to see. The Grand Canyon of armor power.

The Fort Hood motor pool begins at the intersection of Clear Creek Road and North Avenue and runs along the northern edge of the main post that faces the ranges. Bradley fighting vehicles from the First Cavalry Division are parked in rows behind a chain-link fence at the corner. With its swivel turret and cannon, machine guns and Dragon missiles, the Bradley resembles one of those boxy, high-riding tanks from previous eras of warfare, but its main purpose is carrying troops forward in attack. An infantry squad of ten enters through the rear hatch and rides inside while the Bradley focuses its "hunter/killer capacity" on opposing armor.

Six rows of the Bradleys are lined up precisely across the asphalt parking lot. Each tank is painted pale brown, the washed-out color of desert sand, standard decor now for Army combat vehicles.

Heading east, North Avenue dips slightly, and the first lot of Bradleys ends at a drainage ditch. Then there's a new fence, and another motor pool begins. This one is filled with the M-1 Abrams main battle tank, at least two score of them. These particular tanks are designated M-1A2, which indicates that they have been fully upgraded with the latest, most versatile electronics—heat-sensing, eyes-in-the-dark technology, plus a video-display terrain map inside the turret that lets the commander identify every moving object on the battlefield, friend and foe alike.

The M-1 Abrams, named for a revered commander in Vietnam, is without peer in the world—fast and lean despite its tremendous weight, its firepower enhanced by brilliant technological precision. The tank has a low-slung carriage and slender turret, with three machine guns mounted here and there around the 120mm cannon. The low silhouette looks both menacing and sleek, if one can picture seventy tons of sleekness barreling across field and fence rows at thirty-five or forty miles an hour.

"It's like a big old Cadillac with guns," one young tanker told me. A yard filled with them conveys brute authority. There's a small rush in gazing at so much tangible force, assembled in neat, close rows.

Where one parking lot filled with tanks ends, another parking lot filled with tanks begins. Another chain-link fence and another unit's motor pool, more tanks. Then another, then another. More tanks, more tanks. As we drive along North Avenue, reviewing the massed armaments, I ask my escort, Sergeant Troy Rolan, to slow down a bit. I can't take it all in. Sergeant Rolan is amused that I am overwhelmed. The tour is just beginning.

Down the road, another vast parking lot holds a huge fleet of "Humvees" (HMMWV, for High-Mobility Multi-purpose Wheeled Vehicle). These are the squat, wide-body field cars that look as though the designers crossbred an old Jeep with the British Land Rover.

Then come scores of HEMTTs (Heavy Expanded Mobility Tactical Trucks) and HETS (Heavy Equipment Transporter System), the heavy-duty service trucks that support tanks on the battlefield, hauling fuel, ammunition, and even the tanks themselves. "Hemets" are monster freight haulers built for rough terrain. The HETS is a very long, heavy-duty flatbed trailer so strong that it can carry one seventy-ton M-1 tank or two Bradleys.

"It's ridiculously expensive to move these things, so they put them on a HETS and drive them out to the ranges," Sergeant Rolan explains. The rule at Fort Hood is, if a tank has to travel three miles to reach the exercise range, it must be carried piggy-back on a HETS.

Though it sounds a bit silly, this saves real money. A modern battle tank, for all its speed and sophisticated power, is oddly delicate and vulnerable to soaring expenses. An M-1 burns nearly two gallons of fuel per mile. Its tracks and complex operating parts are subject to perpetual wear and breakdown, even from routine travel. Operating a tank in the field, the Army calculates, costs $147 per mile in fuel and repair bills.

Sergeant Rolan drives on, patiently, alongside the massive ribbon of weaponry—more tanks, trucks, cars, Bradleys, armored personnel carriers, Humvees equipped with Avenger missiles, rows of motorized howitzers, fuel tankers, more tanks, more trucks. The sergeant has led this tour before and probably anticipates that there will come a moment when I have had it, when I am so glazed by the experience of seeing all this hardware that I can no longer comprehend one more parking lot of pale-brown combat vehicles.

The moment arrives. It is stirring to look head-on at the mechanical virility of one M-1 battle tank. Seeing several dozen of them, lined up in neat rows, conveys a satisfying sense of power. Trying to look at four or five hundred tanks, immobile across dozens of parking lots, becomes stupefying.

The Fort Hood motor pool finally ends, after forty-eight separate equipment yards, at the entrance to the Hood Army Airfield, where more than two hundred Apache and Kiowa helicopters are stationed. From one end to the other, I have seen something like 2,400 tanks, Bradleys, and other kinds of tracked vehicles—plus more than 11,500 trucks, tankers, Humvees, and other, heavier vehicles on wheels. Exhausting to behold, but there's nothing like it anywhere else in the world. The Fort Hood motor pool stretches along North Avenue for six and a half miles.

◄○►

The parking lots of armor reflect, crudely, the great national dilemma we are evading. America is experiencing a deep confusion of purpose at this moment of history, holding on to a past that is defunct, but unable to imagine a different future. The Cold War is over, but not really, not yet.

Too many tanks with nowhere to send them. Too many bombers and fighter planes, too many ships and rockets. Too many men and women in uniform. Our troops are the best in the world, splendidly trained and capable, brilliantly equipped with dazzling weaponry. But what exactly are they to do, now that a general peace is upon us? We don't know the answer. We don't even want to talk about it.

The defense budget has been reduced since the Berlin Wall came down eight years ago, but $250 billion is still much larger (even after allowing for inflation) than in 1980, the height of Cold War tensions. Overall troop strength has been downsized by roughly one-third, but the nation continues to maintain the heavied-up military force designed and equipped to go head to head against the Soviets. That force structure anticipated a full-scale war waged across the plains of Central Europe—across many of the nations of Central Europe now poised to join NATO.

Fortress America remains mobilized to fight the big one but justifies itself now with vague threat scenarios that envision fighting two wars at once, twin regional conflicts that will be smaller in scale but simultaneous. Instead of a robust debate over new priorities or skeptical questioning of these fanciful premises, the political elites in both parties have settled into denial and drift—a status quo that argues only over smaller matters, like which new weapon systems to fund and where they will be built. Defense spending, as one strategic analyst put it, has become "the new third rail of American politics." Most politicians are afraid to touch it.

It seems improbable that Americans will wish to spend more on a peacetime mobilization, not when federal spending is being cut for nearly everything else. Indeed, the public is inclined right now to stand clear of foreign engagements, especially ones that might involve American casualties. Despite the official projections, most analysts expect defense spending to remain flat or even decline further.

But unwilling or unable to adapt to the new circumstances, the armed forces and their allied manufacturers are proceeding with ambitious plans based on the assumption that the reduction in defense spending is only temporary and that Pentagon budgets will soon begin rising robustly again. (The Clinton administration assumes the same: its five-year projections call for another $30 billion and a 40 percent increase in the procurement budget, while Republicans seek even more.)

Until more money arrives, the defense apparatus is literally feeding on its own parts, pinching this and that, scrimping here and there, in order to keep the same Cold War force structure in place and the same lineup of new weapons moving through the pipeline of development. During the Cold War era, the military institution acquired a reflexive appetite for growth that it's now unwilling to give up. Instead, it lumbers toward a self-induced crisis of malnourishment, as when an addict's starving body eats its own liver.

Some smart people, in and out of the Pentagon, see what's coming and have proposed various blueprints for fundamental restructuring and drastic reduction. Radical alternatives are shrugged off by political and military leaders, however, not to mention the defense industry. It is not necessary to study the mind-numbing budget projections to see the problem. The outlines are visible in the routine facts of military life, the daily burden of maintaining the best and biggest army, navy, and air force in the world.

—◦—

The Pentagon has been dumping old tanks like an army-navy surplus store conducting frantic "going out of business" sales. Giving them away to friendly nations. Selling them at deep discounts. Offering them free to local museums. It dumped one hundred old Sherman M-60s into Mobile Bay off the Alabama coast to form artificial reefs for fish in the Gulf of Mexico. Several hundred more are being sunk along other coastlines for the same purpose. One year it gave forty-five tanks free to Bosnia and another fifty to Jordan. It shipped ninety-one tanks to Brazil under a no-cost, five-year lease, and thirty to Bahrain on the same terms. Another 160 tanks were sold to Taiwan for $130,000 each, priced at ten cents on the dollar. Egypt got seven hundred free by picking up transportation costs.

One way or another, the Army has disposed of nearly six thousand older tanks during the last six years. Giving them away "is often cheaper than destroying or storing them," Lora Lumpe and Paul F. Pineo explained in a 1997 study by the Federation of American Scientists. In the 1980s, they observed dryly, the United States spent many billions on modernizing the Army's entire inventory of armor, helicopters, artillery, and other gear. In the 1990s, it unloaded "a literal army" composed of the same stuff, albeit usually older models. Plus there are the hundreds of "excess" aircraft and ships from the Air Force and Navy inventories.

"The services appear to be giving away still useful equipment in order to justify procurement of new weaponry," Lumpe and Pineo asserted. "Much of the equipment now declared 'excess' is quite serviceable. In fact, a lot of it was purchased or reconditioned in the Reagan arms build-up of the 1980s." These bargain sales have not provoked much controversy, except for occasional complaints from defense firms trying to sell new armaments to the same countries.

12

Redundancy was always a working principle of Cold War weapons procurement—national security based on having more than enough, much more—and that doctrine survives. The Army now holds eleven thousand tanks in its inventory, and nearly all of them are the M-1 Abrams. It's not buying any new ones but is still contracting for technological upgrades on older M-1s. This tank force is at least five or six times larger than those of Iran, Iraq, and North Korea, the "rogue states" most often mentioned in two-war scenarios.

But the U.S. advantage is actually much larger than that because superior technologies multiply the killing strength of our tanks against inferior opponents. Another working principle of Cold War procurement was endless perfectibility—making the standard weapons smarter and smarter. Thanks to its advanced technologies, America designed tanks, planes, ships, and missiles that were far more versatile and precise (also more expensive) than the clunkier mass-produced weapons fielded by the Soviets in larger numbers.

Technology can trump quantity on the modern battlefield. At Fort Hood, Sergeant Major Ronald Coplan, a sixteen-year tank veteran, explains the rough ratios: "The M-1 tank can take out four of any enemy force. An M-1A2 can take out six-to-one." Coplan speaks from practical experience, having driven into Iraq on the leading edge of Desert Storm's devastating tank attack.

Thus, despite the gross reductions, the Army still has too many tanks—at least more than it really needs or can usefully employ. Two MIT political scientists, Harvey M. Sapolsky and Eugene Gholz, have calculated that only about twenty-one hundred tanks—one-fifth of the Army's inventory—are actually deployed and operating with combat divisions. The rest are assigned to reserve units or forward pre-positioning overseas, or they are in storage. The professors found similar redundancy in the Air Force: of seventy-five hundred first-line fighters, only about two thousand were fielded with active units.

The commanders at Fort Hood face a more prosaic problem with the tanks: they can't afford to run them. It costs $2,000 an hour to operate a single M-12A tank in the field. Multiply that by a company with fourteen tanks ($28,000 an hour), a battalion with three or four companies ($84,000 an hour or more), a brigade with three battalions ($252,000 an hour or more), and their problem becomes clear. How can you afford the training hours that soldiers need to operate these brilliant fighting machines?

"This corps, just Fort Hood, will have to operate next year on $80 million less than it did in '96," Colonel School explains. "What can you economize on? Our biggest spending is on training and maintenance. Well, we shift more to simulators and less to actual field training."

To that end, Fort Hood's new Close Combat Tactical Training Center has just been completed. It is a buff-brick warehouse building filled with simulators designed to serve as "virtual tanks" and "virtual Bradley fighting vehicles," even "virtual

14

Humvees." The simulators are thirty-eight windowless metal boxes, each perhaps fifteen feet square, lined up densely inside the vast hall.

A four-man tank crew climbs inside one of these boxes and experiences the authentic interior of an M-1 tank. They "drive" the tank into hostile encounters, "fire" at opposing armor, and get "killed" or "lost" when things go wrong. Afterwards, trainers replay a videotape recording of the action and critique errors.

As in the real thing, the commander sits alongside the breech of the 120mm cannon and faces the usual dials and operating gear, including the electronic terrain map that shows him the battlefield with tiny icons identifying other tanks and units. For visuals, a TV display screen plays a prepared videotape of terrain drawings meant to replicate the fog of battle—generic trees and hills, exploding tanks and helicopter attacks, foot soldiers scurrying for cover, thunder and lightning. The pictures are about as lifelike as an arcade video game.

"If we put one of these machines out there for people to play, we're going to need a boatload of quarters," boasts Lendel W. "Bud" Gotcher, civilian director of Battle Simulations and Systems Integration for the Army. The simulators were built by Lockheed Martin for $670,000 apiece, not counting design and development costs. That's $25 million worth of video games sitting in this arcade.

Bert H. Chole, the site manager for a subcontractor called Pulua Electronics and a retired Army tank commander himself, explains the economics as he shows me in and out of the various simulators.

"These tanks cost a couple of million apiece, and if the Army can save a soldier from tearing them up in training, it makes 'em happy," Chole says. "The bottom line on all this is, it's going to save a lot of damn money. Moving a unit out to the field burns up gasoline and adds to the maintenance. It's simulator miles versus actual field miles. That's the trade-off, and, of course, that's driven by the budget."

In the design room, the two of us look over the shoulder of Sam Kelley, a computer technician who is programming in code changes for a battle scenario the simulator will stage between the "Blue" forces and the "Red" forces. Blue forces are always the good guys in U.S. military training.

"We have an opposing force, and when the friendly forces see it, at that point the interaction will occur," Kelley says. "You'll see fire on the screen, and when it hits, that fire changes the color of the vehicle. Our tanks can shoot farther than their tanks, which are old Warsaw Pact T-64s and T-72s. We could change that. We can give them an enemy fully capable of the same things we can do."

"But we don't have another country like that now," Chole adds. "Believe it or not, the Red forces are programmed according to Soviet threat doctrine. They deploy into the proper defensive formation according to Soviet doctrine. As the Blue forces approach them, certain things happen according to Soviet doctrine. Artillery will come in on 'em, they encounter one or two of our scouts. Then you pick up a Soviet infantry company, then their main line of resistance. That's when the party is really going to fall on you."

Why, I ask, aren't they reprogramming the computers, since the Soviet Union no longer exists? Couldn't the simulators evoke a "virtual enemy" of the future? That would be too expensive, Bert Chole admits.

"We've been working on it for nine years," he explains. "To reprogram it now would be a big trade-off in dollars. How many millions of codes went into this shit? Think of the money it would take to change all of them.

"A reasoning person says, why spend a bunch more money to redesign when, hell, we don't even know who this enemy is? This program will train a force. Let's go with what we got."

Who is chasing us? Or whom do we expect to chase? If their leaders cannot answer that question, it leaves the troops no choice but to prepare to fight an imaginary last war. The dilemma is central. It squeezes all of the military branches into making odd trade-offs between men and machines, between pursuing a real preparedness or a pretend version.

CHAPTER TWO

"BUILT TO FIGHT"

For a moment, the sea becomes a golden glaze as the Navy chopper turns east, flying into the morning sun. The Atlantic Ocean, a couple of thousand feet below, looks empty except for a few specs of flotsam that are fishing boats. Behind us, the Virginia coastline fades from the profile of beachfront hotels and Norfolk's downtown to a watery blur, then disappears.

The pilot is looking for a destroyer, the USS *Arleigh Burke*, which has been out to sea for several days running engineering trials. When he finds it, the *Arleigh Burke* is already steaming homeward. (Although, in fact, there is no steam on this very modern fighting ship; it's turbine-powered by jet engines.) The helicopter makes a wide circle overhead, then swiftly loses altitude to approach the stern. As ship and sea suddenly loom larger, the helo deck looks much smaller, and the helicopter pad is pitching in slow motion with the sea. I come aboard the destroyer with a deeper appreciation for Navy pilots.

Someone hands me a blue ball cap that is standard gear for the 320 crew and officers. The *Arleigh Burke*'s slogan is stitched on the back: "Built to Fight." Indeed it is. Before I can get my sea legs, the combat systems officer, Lieutenant Mike Fulkerson, is leading me off on a brisk, labyrinthine tour of the weaponry.

Along the narrow passageways, stepping through bulkhead doors, we scramble chest to chest past working sailors and skitter down the steep ladder stairs. From the engine room to the bridge, the ship is six stories of dense steelwork. What looked from the air like a slender gray vessel with a laid-back silhouette is a complex package of long-range destruction.

"I carry ninety missiles on board, and I can mix and match those," Fulkerson says as we inspect boxlike missile tubes in the bowels of the ship. "I can put ninety Tomahawks or standard surface-to-air missiles or antisubmarine rockets in any of those ninety holes."

The next moment, Fulkerson is scrambling up more stairs and outside along the railing of the main deck, then up another flight to the missile deck, where the rows of heavy-duty manhole covers are missile caps that open at launching. Resting against the ship's superstructure are the sloped cradles that hold the much larger Harpoon missiles, which Fulkerson can target across hundreds of miles, plus two sets of torpedo tubes alongside.

The destroyer is fitted with the Aegis weapons system, but it still carries the traditional naval armament—a monster five-inch gun up front. It seems antique—and redundant—alongside everything else. So does the 20mm Gatling gun with six revolving barrels. "That's for close-range self-defense," the lieutenant explains. "It fires three thousand rounds a minute. The gun tracks incoming missiles and tracks the outgoing bullets and then adjusts the two on top of each other."

The real action, if it should occur, will be down below in the Combat Information Center, a large room of shaded light and glowing video screens, men staring at computer monitors and keyboards. A giant electronic display map overhead depicts the Virginia coast in red and identifies other ships and air traffic in the vicinity. The training tape that's playing shows the *Arleigh Burke* firing at an approaching aircraft.

"The old days of the captain going up to the bridge to fight the ship are long gone," Fulkerson explains. "It's all too fast. Everything happens here. The captain sits here next to the tactical action officer." There are two TV cameras mounted outside to scan the horizon and provide the combat technicians with a video glimpse of the sea.

Captain Mark Kosnik is a slightly built man with a full mustache and a big boyish smile, wearing a blue windbreaker and ball cap. "I've got the best job in the world really," the captain says. "I've worked twenty years to be in charge of something, and I'm having a wonderful time. What makes me feel very good is that the Navy has invested in this type of ship. The technology allows this ship to do anything a small combatant ship needs to do."

His ship was commissioned in 1991—the first one in a new destroyer class that is also named for Arleigh Burke, a legendary admiral who made his name in World War II leading daring destroyer raids on Japanese warships. The Arleigh Burke destroyer efficiently incorporates myriad high-tech innovations and more firepower but is slightly smaller and faster (top speed thirty-one knots) than the older destroyers it replaces. "You can't make an 8,500-ton destroyer 'stealth,' but they made a lot of design changes to make us a smaller blip on the enemy's radar screen," Fulkerson says.

The Navy has acquired seventeen Arleigh Burke–class destroyers since 1991 and intends to buy another twelve, priced at $850 million each. For the moment, however, the new destroyers are held hostage by a hardball political squabble over just where they should be built. The Navy had originally assigned all of the work to General Dynamics' Bath Iron Works in Maine, a decision that pleased Maine Senator William Cohen, an influential Republican on military issues. Since then, however, Cohen has retired from the Senate and become secretary of Defense.

Another powerful Republican, Senate Majority Leader Trent Lott of Mississippi, is upset about the work going to Maine. Lott has watched the Ingalls Shipyard at Pascagoula, Mississippi, lose Navy projects and dwindle from seventeen thousand to ten thousand workers. He suggests, none too subtly, that Mississippians can build an Arleigh Burke as good as Maine's. The Navy gets the message. It now proposes to share the work fifty-fifty between the two states. But its capitulation to politics still must be cleared by the Defense secretary from Maine.

Put aside the politics, however, and the weapons technology. The most arresting impression of this ship is formed by the men who operate it (no women aboard yet, though that's coming). A cliché common to all three military services holds that the people matter more than the machines, and in fundamental ways it's true.

Up on the bridge, perched fifty-five feet above the waterline, an officer calls out the headings, but the helm is in the hands of a twenty-seven-year-old bosun's mate, Eddie Lamon of Orlando, Florida. "It's fun sometimes when we're doing drills and there's heavy action," he says. Steering a 502-foot-long ship on a steady course is harder than it looks. (I know, I tried for a moment.) Like a sailboat skipper, the helmsman is continuously correcting for wind and sea, but if he overcorrects, it sends the ship veering in an equal, opposite direction. Then he must correct again for his own mistake.

Today a younger seaman, a tall blond kid named Tom Mullikin from a small town outside of Columbus, Ohio, is at Lamon's side, watching and listening. Later in the day, when the ship is about to reenter the Norfolk harbor through the mouth of Chesapeake Bay, Mullikin will be given the helm to steer down the narrow channel. If he doesn't mess up, he completes his training as a master helmsman.

"I was working a dead-end factory job back home, cutting fabric for car seats," he says. "Now I'm here forever, at least for the next couple of years." He is twenty-one. "Tell you the truth, it's boring sometimes, when everything is calm and clear," Mullikin says. "But it's fun to steer up when it's rocking and rolling."

Six decks below in the engine room, a wall panel has been removed, revealing one of the four GE jet engines (equivalent to a DC-10's) that power the ship's twin shafts. Three young sailors are squatting inside the engine compartment, on their hands and knees or backs, repairing the fluted metalwork that covers the engine's carcass. "We got one guy watching and a couple of salty dogs doing the actual work," jokes Roger McCormack, the engine room's senior chief.

The "salty dog" who's in charge slides out from under the engine and turns out to be twenty-two years old. Petty Officer Eddie Ramirez from Los Angeles is in blue coveralls, with a lean, brown face and a smudge of grease on his brow.

"I'm mechanically minded," Ramirez says, "but I really learned all this hands-on mostly. Many hours of practice, working with the technical manual in your hand. The Navy's taught me just about everything I know since I was a kid, since I came in at seventeen. I got five guys working for me now. I'm responsible for three engines."

As he wipes off his hands, the shy deference recedes. "You know," he volunteers, "I'm putting in for officer training. You know about the 'Seaman to Admiral' program, right? I'm applying." Does he want to become an admiral someday? Not really, he says. "Number one, I want an education. Number two, it's like payback time. The Navy did for me. I'm going to do for the Navy. I'm not staying for twenty years, but I'm going to do good work while I'm here."

During my hop-skip tour of military bases, I have had numerous encounters with people like Ramirez—capable young men and women, some very young, who are doing highly complex work, with enormous responsibility riding on getting it right. Some are bored with the repetitious routines, and some chafe at having to follow dumb orders from higher rank. But many recount how military service opened up their lives and altered their sense of their own potential.

At Fort Hood, I was cramped down inside the belly of an M-1 tank with a pink-cheeked Iowa boy named Damion Peters. He is a twenty-three-year-old sergeant and the crew chief for a battalion commander. "This is the CO's tank," Sergeant Peters says, "but really I think of it as my tank. I'm the one who signs for it, I'm the one responsible for its upkeep. And they wouldn't have given me this tank if I hadn't earned it."

After a year in college, where he got heavily into the party scene, Peters enlisted in the Army, partly for the $17,000 tuition aid, partly because his dad had served before him. "I built my self esteem big time," he says. "You learn to do things right, and they'll let you know if you're wrong." He served in Germany and loved traveling around Europe, but he plans to get out and go back to school, maybe become an accountant.

Back down in the *Arleigh Burke's* engine room, Chief McCormack describes the implications for poor or working-class kids with limited prospects. "A lot of these young guys go home on leave and they see their friends working in a supermarket or bar, maybe the Wal-Mart, while they've just been in the Bahamas," McCormack explains. "When you're seventeen, eighteen years old, you've got a whole world out there to see, and they're doing something real with their lives, not just locked into the same old thing every day for forty years."

Whatever else it achieves, the military institution serves as an important social ladder in American life—a real opening for kids who lack the usual advantages but aspire to advance themselves. That social reality provides another, subtler reason for politicians' reluctance to restructure the military force in dramatic ways. Shrinking the force structure, they know, will take the ladder away, with nothing much to replace it in domestic life.

It is, however, an expensive ladder to maintain. Operating the *Arleigh Burke,* for instance, costs about $30,000 a day, or $11.3 million a year, according to the Navy, plus another $1.8 million devoted solely to various training activities. In fact, when you think about it, the training of people is what the Navy mainly does—that and keeping the equipment working. (The same can be said for the Army and the Air Force.)

At the officers' mess, Captain Kosnik and Lieutenant Commander Kevin Sweeney, the ship's executive officer, are mulling over the uncertain future. Both are Naval Academy graduates who started their career in flusher times. "When I graduated from the academy in '82, things were fat and getting fatter," the EXO recalls. "Budgets were growing, we were going to a 600-

ship navy, the sky was the limit." The Navy peaked just short of 600 active ships and has since shrunk to about 350.

"There are fewer opportunities now to move up because the ships are so much fewer," the captain explains. "In fact, the last time I had a couple of questions—is there going to be another drawdown?—I had to be honest. I don't know what's going to happen. But the budgets are tough, and there's going to be more tightening."

Some restructuring proposals suggest that the Navy can mothball large numbers of ships, keep them in ready reserve at much lower cost, and reactivate them if a real war develops. Kevin Sweeney is skeptical. "You can't do that with combatants," he insists. "You've seen it, it's all high-tech. You can't just throw in a humidifier and walk away. It will all deteriorate."

While the *Arleigh Burke* can expect to survive downsizing pressures, everyone wonders about the larger impact on officers and crew. "There's a minimum point somewhere that you can't go below, particularly in our game," Sweeney suggests. "You have to have the people prepared to be deployed. But if you take away a chunk of the force structure, then you drive people out of the service because they don't want to go out for nine-month deployments. We made that commitment in the Navy—not to go above six-month deployments. So what do we do? Do we make the battle groups a little smaller?"

To maintain a high state of readiness, destroyers follow an eighteen-month cycle—twelve months in homeport training, six months deployed overseas with a battle group, with three months in the shipyard for repairs. Then back home and the cycle repeats itself. During the training phase, the ship gets to sea only twenty-seven days or so each quarter, but twice as much during deployments. With the computerized weapons systems, officers and crew do a lot of simulated practice without going anywhere. "We can sit pierside in Norfolk and be in the Persian Gulf," Captain Kosnik says.

But high-tech details aside, the core of the routine is about prepping people who pass through in the normal turnover of personnel.

"All we really care about is training these young guys so they can qualify to move up the ladder," Sweeney says. "It's a continuous process. You come in as an ensign and qualify to serve as a line officer or department head, then hope to come back as EXO and finally commander. We're worrying about young guys getting trained and qualified to move up. That's what we do day in and day out, to tell the truth."

His explanation leaves me pondering the Navy's dilemma: it is like the shark that never sleeps, that must keep moving through the water, feeding continuously to sustain itself. The same training dilemma confronts all of the armed services. If you slow down the cycle too much or short-change it, if military readiness is reduced to computerized simulations, then the people moving through the system may not get what they need to operate the high-technology armaments. But if you try to keep everyone fully primed for war, in perpetuity, it's so expensive that something has to be sacrificed.

The military is not a shark, of course. More like a whale.

By late afternoon, the ship is nearly home, and Tom Mullikin is at the helm, looking cool and vigilant, with the hint of a sheepish smile at the corners of his mouth. The *Arleigh Burke* has slowed to fifteen knots, and Mullikin is steering down the Thimble Shoal Channel into Chesapeake Bay. Nearly all of the ship's twenty-two officers are on the bridge, scanning the horizon for anything the officer of the bridge might not see. The navigation team is taking visual sightings and recalculating the ship's position every few seconds. The radar system backs them up.

The weather is mild, and the passage seems utterly routine, but there's still a sense of alert exhilaration on the bridge. For people on ships, this two-lane channel can be dangerous, especially in foul weather or at night. Even on a sunny afternoon, it is great fun to steer a destroyer back home.

As it enters the bay, the ship makes a left hook toward the Navy yard at Norfolk. A harbor pilot comes aboard to supervise the two Navy tugs that will nudge the *Arleigh Burke* backwards into its berth. The feeling is triumphal as the ship glides slowly past the fleet—alongside dozens of warships at pierside, main elements of the Atlantic Fleet. Three aircraft carriers are in port and loom over everything else, the frigates and cruisers, combat store ships, oilers, a submarine in dry dock, ten other destroyers. Nothing like it anywhere else in the world.

Far across the bay, one can glimpse the gigantic cranes of the Newport News shipyard, where eighteen thousand workers are building more ships for the Navy. Newport News Shipbuilding Company is the largest private employer in Virginia. A new aircraft carrier, the *Harry S. Truman,* priced at $4.5 billion, is assembled and sits at dockside getting its final fittings. Next year, the keel will be laid for another new carrier, the *Ronald Reagan,* which is likely to cost $5 billion. Does anyone dare ask whether America actually needs this aircraft carrier called *Ronald Reagan?*

CHAPTER THREE

RED FLAGS
OVER NEVADA

THE SQUADRON OF F-16S PREPARES FOR TAKEOFF WITH A HIGH WHINE THAT BUILDS TO GENERAL THUNDER AS THEY GATHER SPEED DOWN THE runway. One after another, as the fighters pass by us, the distinctive needle-nose lifts up, then the sleek F-16 is in the air. The beautiful bird trails a loud aftershock that abruptly pounds your chest. Moments later, the squadron arranges itself and disappears over the mountain ridge to the north.

Then the roar begins again—more F-16s taking off—only this time they are on both sides of us. Two squadrons are launching simultaneously on the parallel runways at Nellis Air Force Base, as if racing to become airborne. Staff Sergeant James Brooks has parked the military pickup truck at a midpoint between the two runways so that we can have a physically intimate experience of the show.

During the next half hour, we watch sixty-two aircraft take off and fly north. (Actually, they depart so rapidly, I lose count.) More than three dozen F-16s, including a squadron designated as the "aggressors"—eight of the twin-tailed F-15s. An EF-111 fighter-bomber equipped for electronics warfare. A lumbering AWACS with its huge radar disc on top, four Marine Harriers, two C-130 transports, plus assorted other aircraft. From Las

Vegas, they head somewhere over the Nevada desert for an afternoon of "live fly" aerial combat.

Of course, we cannot observe the actual battle, since the planes are spread across airspace 120 miles long and 60 miles wide, and they are traveling at 400–500 miles an hour. The closest we get to the action is in a darkened theater where the high-speed, low-altitude engagements play out in slow motion on a huge multidimensional electronic map. The Blue Force is attacking from the east—triangular blue icons moving toward their bombing targets—while the Red team defends "the motherland" from the west.

Red fighters fly out to challenge the F-16 strikers and lead them on a chase. F-15s, the green icons, fly at higher altitude and are also engaged in air-to-air combat. EF-111s penetrate close enough to excite the enemy's radar and jam it, identifying the location of air defense missiles the F-16s will take out.

As the mock battle unfolds, the map becomes a confused mix of blue and red icons swarming this way and that at different altitudes. The hits and misses are only electronic, scored by two committees of impartial judges known as the "Showtime Guys." "Cyclone 1, you're dead," a radio transmission from Showtime announces. No response from the F-15. "Cyclone 1, you're dead." "Yeah, I copy," a sullen voice replies. The plane climbs to twenty-five hundred feet and exits the air space.

During the exercise I'm following, the judges rule that four F-15s are "lost" in air-to-air combat and three other Blue Force aircraft are brought down by ground fire. But the Red team loses ten planes and the Blue team "destroys" 70 percent of its bombing targets. Afterwards, the pilots gather in debriefings to critique performance and tactics.

Short of the real thing, this is probably as good as it gets. The Air Force has been staging its "Red Flag exercises" at Nellis since the 1970s to replicate the experience of air combat, with increasing elements of realism. The entire range covers 12,000 square miles, including 50 "Red surface threats" that are manned and shoot back. For live ordnance, 1,400 targets are situated across 935,500 acres of "bombable range."

Real MIGs are no longer employed as Red Force aggressors, but several squadrons of U.S. aircraft are painted in the sky-blue or mottled-brown camouflage patterns used by the Soviet Union and some Middle East nations. Now that the Cold War is over, the Red Flag Center leases old Soviet helicopters and fixed-wing aircraft from the Russian government for added verisimilitude.

For two weeks of training at Nellis, pilots, ground crews, and aircraft have been gathered from Tinker Air Force Base in Oklahoma, Cannon in New Mexico, Shaw in South Carolina, Eglin in Florida, and Luke in Arizona. Red Flag is so popular that twenty-one foreign military services have sent their planes and pilots to experience it, too, from Germany and Britain to Brazil and Indonesia, even Thailand and Singapore. Low-level flying creates unpopular noise problems across Europe, but America has open space in abundance. Nellis Air Force Base is about the size of Connecticut.

Foreign governments must pay for the privilege because Red Flag is naturally expensive. An hour's flying time in an F-16 costs about $2,500, an F-15 nearly $5,000. Five or six times a year, Nellis stages a six-week program of exercises, with different squadrons rotating in and out. It costs $2.2 million to run each one, the base estimates.

The combat feels real, but the threat is a bit confused. The Red Force now follows a mix of tactical doctrines, including the old fighting style of Soviet MIGs, which are now widely owned around the world. But some potential adversaries also fly French and Italian planes, even U.S. aircraft. Iran, for one, has American-made F-4s and F-14s. "Those guys got trained in Western-style tactics," Major Steve Face explains as we watch the battle map. "So their tactics could be totally different from guys trained in a Soviet schoolhouse."

At a briefing for visiting notables, Colonel F. F. "Fack" Acker, vice commander of the Fifty-seventh Wing, gives a bracing account of why the Air Force must acquire the new F-22 fighter plane to counter "what we think the next generation of threat will be." Dressed in an olive-drab jumpsuit, boots, and checkered scarf, the colonel has the lean, square-shouldered look of a proud pilot. His tone is grave as he strides back and forth before the audience, describing the training needed to meet the "full-on threat." Finally, one visitor asks: "Who exactly are you talking about?"

"Look at a map of the world," Colonel Acker says. "You see the Chinese making upgrades. The Koreans making upgrades. You look at the Middle East. . . . Saddam is upgrading and filling the holes. You just can't predict. People we think are friends. The Brits in the Falklands. Thought they were okay, and they took it on the chin for the first ten or fifteen days."

But, he's asked, can any of those nations really pose a challenge to U.S. military power?

"I agree with you," the colonel says. "There is no one place that, if we went full out, one on one, we couldn't go there and kick their you-know-what. Take care of business, if that's what the president and secretary of Defense want us to do. But we don't know what kind of coalitions they're developing among themselves and how they might develop in the future."

"Who is 'they'? That's a good question," Lieutenant Colonel Virgil Unger, the Red Flag vice commander, reflects in conversation afterwards. "You knew then who it was. Now it could be anything."

"We knew it was the bear, and we had a purpose," Colonel Bill Rake, the Red Flag commander, says wistfully, as if nostalgic for the simpler times. "We did the training for the bear. Now the bear might not be there. But somebody might just jump up from behind the door. Iran, Iraq? We don't know."

The absence of well-defined doctrine leaves commanders to imagine an impossible task—equipping expeditionary forces to oppose an unknowable future, wherever and whatever it turns up. The military senses an obvious danger in this open-ended and ill-defined assignment: they have not been told very clearly what to get ready for, but they know they will be held accountable if they have failed to prepare.

The quandary dogs everything these men and their fliers are expected to accomplish, but this quandary really belongs to the nation. The bear gave us purpose. But what is the purpose of all this now that the bear is gone?

◄○►

The Air Force faces the same internal tensions and contradictions that are present in the Navy and Army, but, if anything, its problems are more visible. An exaggerated redundancy of killing power versus the industrial plans to build more—another generation of newer, smarter, more expensive weapons systems. The need to downsize and economize versus the costly realities of continuous training for the people who must operate high-tech weaponry. The pride and opportunities of military life versus the stress and insecurities that peace has imposed on people in uniform.

At Nellis, the personal stress is a staple of conversation—separation and divorce, stalled careers, frequent overseas deployments, drinking and depression, uncertainty about the future. The distress symptoms are alarming enough to prompt the base to circulate a medical bulletin on "suicide awareness."

Since 1990, suicide has been the second leading cause of death for active-duty Air Force members (unintentional injuries were first), the Ninety-ninth Medical Group reported in 1997. One should not exaggerate the import of this statistic, since the rate of successful suicides per thousand remains relatively low. Still, the rate has increased by two-thirds since the late 1980s.

> The suicide rate among members between ages twenty and twenty-nine has increased drastically. . . . The most common cause for suicide is difficulty in a relationship (breakup, divorce, or separation) or family problems. . . . Difficulties at work are the second most common cause. . . . Enlisted personnel are more likely to commit suicide. . . . Most suicides occur during the summer in conjunction with permanent change-of-station moves or family separation.

Out on the airfield's ramp, where more than one hundred fighter planes are parked for the exercises, Sergeant Brooks and I amble from squadron to squadron, chatting with airmen in the ground crews. The sergeant encounters several old buddies from his previous assignments in New Mexico and England. They congratulate him on his recent promotion and commiserate over his recent marital separation. Sergeant Brooks seems a sweetly conscientious man, hardworking and a bit harried by multiple obligations at work and at home.

"What's kind of sad," he confides afterwards, "is all three of those guys have been divorced, and now it looks like I'm headed the same way."

37

Service men and women go through the same family tensions as anyone else in America, but with the added complication of long periods of separation during the deployments. As U.S. force strength is reduced overseas, it means more trips abroad for some units, particularly the ones with specialized skills like military police or electronic surveillance.

"When I get back home from here, I go right back to Saudi," says Technical Sergeant Ken Oswald, who is thirty-five years old and works on the EF-111s that flew from Clovis, New Mexico. "Since 1990, we've been going and going. This'll be my seventh time in Saudi. I've got almost 230 days gone last year between Saudi and Turkey."

He's not complaining. This is the duty. But it does get tiresome. "You're living in a tent out there for anywhere from ninety to a hundred days at a time," Sergeant Oswald says. "The only contact you get with home is a 'morale call' once a week."

The family pays a price, too. "I got three boys who play soccer and basketball, and my wife just tries to keep things going," he says. "That's the worst part. You miss a lot of their growing up."

For fighter pilots, the frequent deployment to various peace-keeping missions—like patrolling the "no-fly zones" over Iraq—creates a different sort of frustration. Flying lazy circles in the sky is not what these guys were trained to do. "It lulls you into a sense of complacency," Colonel Rake explains. "A pilot is like a race car driver trained to race at 180 miles per hour. Then you tell him to drive 25 miles per hour."

38

The reckless bravado of fighter pilots is an outdated legend since the skills are now much more cerebral. Technology has reduced many uncertainties of doing air battle at high speeds, but exquisitely attuned mental reflexes are still required. "As a rule of thumb, you think a minute ahead of your aircraft," says Colonel Unger. "If you're going 480 miles per hour, that's eight miles a minute, so you need to think eight to ten miles downstream from where you are."

This is fun as well as dangerous. Captain Bob "Animal" Sowers gets such a kick from his job that he's hanging on as long as he can; he's been flying fighters for thirteen years. In his midthirties and passed over for major, now he flies the second seat in an EF-III. The budget squeeze is closing in on that aircraft, too.

"We're the only jamming aircraft in the Air Force, and there's only one squadron of us, and everybody wants us for their mission," Sowers says. "But now the Navy EA-6s are going to take over our function. I'd go back to England in a minute, but there's nowhere to go. I'd go anyplace in Europe, but there's not much left. I'd even switch to the Navy."

A lot of other pilots are getting out, but the prospect depresses Captain Sowers. "I'm getting paid $60,000 a year to do what I really enjoy," he says. "You're not likely to beat that on the outside. The thought of just ferrying someone back and forth in a private jet from Albuquerque to Las Vegas—that's like driving a bus to me."

◄○►

Obsolescence threatens the machines as well as the people. If one is to believe the Pentagon's claims, America's frontline fighter plane, the F-15, is destined to become outmoded and must be replaced. Like the M-1 tank or the Arleigh Burke destroyer, the F-15 has no peer anywhere in the world, but a new, even more versatile aircraft goes into production next year.

This spring, Lockheed Martin rolled out the first model of the F-22 at its plant in Marietta, Georgia, and staged an official celebration of the plane that is said to ensure "air dominance" in the twenty-first century. The F-22 was conceived and designed in the 1980s to meet the Soviet threat that Pentagon planners projected for the mid-1990s. And so it will, despite the awkward fact that the Soviet Union no longer exists.

Each F-22 will cost $161 million (assuming the cost estimates are accurate and honest), and the Air Force wants to buy around 438 of them, a future commitment of $70 billion.

The Navy, meanwhile, is replacing its aircraft, too. The new F/A-18 E/F fighter-bombers, to be built by Boeing, will cost $80 million each—a lot less than the F-22, but the Navy intends to buy 1,000 of them, a commitment of $80 billion.

The Army, for its part, has a $45 billion program under way to acquire 1,292 new Commanche armed reconnaissance helicopters.

The armed services are together also purchasing $76 billion in precision-guided bombs plus new equipment for air defense and close artillery support. That's roughly $300 billion in better weaponry for the future. But there's more.

The Air Force, Navy, and Marine Corps are collaborating on the creation of the Joint Strike Fighter (JSF), a swept-wing aircraft so versatile it will fill the future tactical needs of all three services, even the vertical takeoff capacity the Marines want. A competition is under way among the major defense contractors, Lockheed Martin, Boeing, and others, to see who will win this prize. The stakes are huge, since total acquisition costs are likely to exceed $300 billion. A decade from now, when the JSF rolls out, the services promise to buy 2,978 of them.

Before any of these new weapons systems are produced, however, another awkward fact still stalks the Air Force, Army, and Navy: the excess of lethality that exists right now. Even if one takes seriously the scenarios for fighting two wars at once, the armed services have a surplus of killing power. Gross reductions have been made—tanks, ships, and planes removed from the active inventory. But a lot of new stuff has also been purchased. Procurements that were planned in the Cold War days rolled forward anyway, after the bear's demise.

Since 1991, the General Accounting Office (GAO) calculates, the Pentagon has tripled its inventory of long-range missiles to attack ground targets (and upgraded many older missiles). After the Cold War ended, the government added 2,662 Tomahawks and other missiles to its arsenal. It increased air power capabilities by modernizing 961 night-capable aircraft and 707 precision-guided munitions-capable aircraft.

The Air Force has so many long-range bombers—the old reliable B-52, the troubled B-1, the new, stealthy B-2 that costs $2 billion apiece—that it cannot afford to keep them all in the air. Yet, if you can believe its plans, the Air Force intends to increase the operational bomber force 25 percent by 2001.

The B-1 bomber is the Cold War's most celebrated white elephant. I saw some in training at Ellsworth Air Force Base in South Dakota and felt sympathy for the dilemma of pilots and commanders there. The nation spent hundreds of billions building and deploying one hundred B-1s. (Four have since crashed.) The plane is designed for intercontinental nuclear strikes deep inside the Soviet Union, a mission that no longer exists. They are being converted to conventional bombs but were not sent to the Gulf War.

The B-1's charter is reduced to flying occasional "global power missions," whatever that means. Because they are so expensive to operate, twenty-seven of the B-1 fleet were put in "reconstitution reserve status." That is, they have no crews assigned to fly them. However, the Air Force intends to activate them again as soon as it can find the money.

Bottom line: a staggering target overkill exists in Fortress America, even for fighting two wars at once. The GAO has documented the redundancies in a 1996 study:

The services already have at least 10 ways to hit 65 percent of the thousands of expected ground targets in two major regional conflicts. In addition, service interdiction assets can provide 140 to 160 percent coverage for many types of targets. Despite their numerous overlapping, often redundant, interdiction capabilities, the services plan to acquire aircraft and other weapons over the next 15 to 20 years that will further enhance their interdiction capabilities.

All these contradictions collide in the defense budget. The newly balanced federal budget does not help because the Pentagon, like everything else, has a strict ceiling imposed on its spending. Its weapons procurement budget declined sharply after the Cold War ended, but everyone knows it must now increase sharply if the services are to acquire all of the new weaponry they are committed to buy. Any rise in procurement spending will require deep cuts in the competing accounts—training, maintenance, and personnel. But if training and operations are cut further, how do we maintain a fighting force that is ready to fight? And what happens to the morale of men and women in uniform as their duties are stretched further and their ladder for promotion keeps shrinking?

The operative solution to these questions is to avoid facing them—to push the hard choices further and further off into the future. Each year, the new Department of Defense budget projects that "next year" or in subsequent years the financial squeeze will be magically resolved by increased spending. When next year arrives, the same prediction is repeated.

After all, there is always the dim hope that somehow the circumstances will change. Who knows, maybe the Cold War will start again. Maybe North Korea will invade South Korea. Maybe China will turn belligerent. The nation's political and military leaders seem to be searching forlornly for a "they" that can restore purpose to the country's mighty armaments.

The military establishment, therefore, marches forward to meet itself in financial crisis. This year, Secretary of Defense Cohen undertook a quadrennial "bottom-up review" that was supposed to ask the fundamental question: How much is enough in a time of general peace? Neither the Clinton administration nor the Republican Congress has the stomach for that kind of confrontation with reality. So, instead, Cohen decided to stay with the two-wars threat scenario. That left him to devise the smaller choices and nasty trade-offs that will push the larger dilemma off again until "next year." The Air Force decided, for instance, to sacrifice people in order to hang on to future weaponry. Another 25,000 or 30,000 service men and women were cut to pay for the F-22. But the Defense secretary needed still more savings. So he reduced the number of F-22s that the Air Force would be allowed to buy in the future, from 438 to 339. Instead of buying 1,000 modernized F-18s, the Navy was told it will get far fewer.

The paradox in all these choices comes down to this: America's ability to field the more highly advanced armaments may save some personnel at risk on the battlefield or in the air, but it doesn't save money. In fact, the supporting forces, from technicians to repair mechanics, must be much deeper for high-tech warfare. And the training required for the men and women who have to operate the weaponry becomes still more demanding as weapons are upgraded and reinvented.

America made the strategic choice to go with high-tech weaponry during the Cold War rivalry, and it is not likely to undo the decision now. But the cost of sustaining this armament system in peacetime—training high-tech warriors while building new, more complex machines—creates a profound collision between the warriors and the machines. In a sense, they are competing with each other for the money.

The procurement and manpower cuts help to balance the Pentagon's bookkeeping, but they also automatically raise the per-unit cost of producing each aircraft. The price tags cited above are too low. Each F-22 is actually going to cost more than $161 million, and the F-18s are going to cost more than $80 million apiece. The military managers can patch together short-term budget fixes, but pushing the larger dilemma of national defense further into the future does not resolve it. It simply makes it harder and more expensive to confront the issue someday.

The juggernaut—the best and biggest military force in the world—lumbers on, doing what it knows how to do best. It is unwilling to rethink its future, unable to let go of the past. Like the shark, it must keep feeding, only now it is feeding on itself.

PART
II

◄○►

CHAPTER FOUR

BRIDGE TO THE 21ST CENTURY

The huge industrial barn on the west side of Fort Worth seems endless, viewed from the parking lot out front. The factory is six stories tall and windowless. The corrugated siding, painted sand brown, glows in the morning sun and goes on for a mile or more. When the factory was built a half-century ago, it was said to be the largest air-conditioned building in the world.

Across the street is a row of two dozen hangars and the 13,500-foot runway where new fighter planes are flight-tested. The factory used to share this airstrip with Carswell Air Force Base across the way, but Carswell was closed after the Cold War ended. The factory lives on, still turning out F-16s, the Fighting Falcon. The contractor is Lockheed Martin, but the factory is called Air Force Plant 4 since it was built and owned by the U.S. government. Indeed, it is still owned by the nation's taxpayers, though they collect no rent on their building. Air Force Plant 4 is one of the many places where America's military-industrial complex was born.

Large portions of Plant 4 are quite gloomy now—emptied of machines and people. But it's still producing military aircraft, and no one in management expects that to end. Before we go inside, let's look at the larger story that Air Force Plant 4 tells us about the rise of the U.S. arms industry—where it came from and why it remains so powerful in the midst of peace.

This factory began at a heroic moment in the national experience. The Japanese bombed Pearl Harbor on December 7, 1941, and Americans were suddenly pulled into World War II with a mobilizing anger. Five months later, the bomber plant was completed at Fort Worth and already producing the B-24 bomber, the Liberator, in prodigious numbers. The B-24 may not have been the most celebrated aircraft of the war, but it was a reliable workhorse. Waves of them bombed the beach cliffs at Normandy before dawn to soften up German defenses for the D-Day invasion. They led the opening raid in the decisive destruction of Berlin.

Fort Worth turned out more than three thousand Liberators and had thirty thousand employees at peak production. One-third of the workers were women. The legend of "Rosie the Riveter" seems quaint, even slightly sexist, by present standards, but it presaged the fundamental social change that we now know as feminism. More than eleven million men were in uniform, gone to war. Somebody had to build the ships and tanks and airplanes. Black Americans, still a segregated underclass, were also admitted to many prime industrial jobs. This opening stoked their thirst for equality and helped inspire the civil rights movement that followed the war.

People around Fort Worth say that, when Plant 4 was really humming, a new bomber would be rolled out *every hour.* When new planes went up for their maiden flight, some of them still had workers inside, finishing off the interiors. This sounds at first like exaggeration, but not when one looks at the old black-and-white photographs of Plant 4's assembly line. Dozens of bombers are lined up wing to wing in a double row that stretches back through the vast hall, farther than the camera can see. Scores of machinists are scrambling over wings and fuselage, in and out of hatches.

World War II was like that. On the home front, a dramatic surge of productive energy was unleashed, along with profound social change. There was plenty of discord, but the war mobilization produced a muscular sense of national unity that may seem quaint to alienated citizens of the 1990s. People and business enterprises put aside cars, houses, and refrigerators, shifted rapidly to war production, and, in the process, transformed the national economy. In the 1930s, Americans had staggered through a decade of impoverishing depression. Force-fed by the government's new spending on weapons, the U.S. economy grew in size during the war years by an astonishing 75 percent.

The necessities of winning, plus many billions in government subsidy, created the new industrial base and the new technologies (aerospace, petrochemicals, electronics, and others) upon which U.S. postwar prosperity in the 1950s and 1960s was built. In economic terms, World War II was a model of what was possible if Americans ever got their act together, if they ever again achieved consensus on the national purpose.

The war also created the mixed marriage of government and private enterprise that is with us still: a huge and diverse manufacturing sector dedicated to serving one customer—the Department of Defense. It includes thousands of small and medium-sized firms and a handful of mammoth corporations that are the prime contractors. All are deeply dependent on politics to fill their order books.

President Dwight D. Eisenhower, the general who commanded the military victory over Hitler, labeled it the "military-industrial complex" and warned against its encroaching influence. Critics later coined an ominous metaphor—the Iron Triangle—to explain its political power. The three sides of the triangle are formed by Congress, the defense companies, and the military leadership—three power centers that interact to reinforce their mutual interests: jobs, contracts, new weaponry.

When other nations employ such tactics to advance their own economic development, American commentators typically deride the arrangement as "state socialism" and warn that it will generate wasteful inefficiencies and entrenched interests that will become very difficult to dislodge. The U.S. arms industry has done both (while also spawning spectacular innovations in the technologies of war-making), but conservatives do not put a socialist label on the government-business marriage that supports the arms industry since it serves the high purpose of defending the nation. And in industrial terms, the nation never truly demobilized after World War II. Scores of the major factories and shipyards that Washington had built for contractors to operate remained in place, though producing at much lower levels. (Fifty years later, the government still owns more than sixty of those factories, and they are still operated by private firms.)

The shock of Pearl Harbor left a political conviction that the United States must never be caught flatfooted again. Keep the defense industrial base "warm," ready to make new weapons again, just in case. After 1948, when Cold War was joined with the Soviets, arms production flourished anew. The ensuing five decades of permanent war mobilization have been an era unlike any other time in American history.

Nor does the government intend to demobilize now that the Soviet Union has expired. An industrial sector devoted to making superior weapons, from fighter planes to nuclear missiles to high-tech electronics warfare, is regarded as a commercial triumph and a national treasure. It's hard to recall that America once got along without it.

If one visualizes the up-and-down history of this industrial installation, it can be understood as a rough metaphor for the entire defense industry. The present predicament of Plant 4 in Fort Worth illustrates a complex business story that is quite different from what's been conveyed about arms makers in the last few years. The weapons companies have undergone a dramatic and painful downsizing and corporate consolidation. But the restructuring is actually a big disappointment for taxpayers.

53

Despite the changes, the industry remains wildly oversized in its capacity to produce new weaponry; too many factories are waiting for the next war. These circumstances put enormous political pressure on their customer—the U.S. government—to keep buying more new stuff it doesn't really need. But the excess capacity also generates a new kind of arms race among the competing companies themselves, here and abroad.

The awesome industrial base that America built to win World War II and then the Cold War has now emerged as the premier arms merchant to the world. With our government's encouragement and subsidy, the industry sells advanced U.S. weapons to developing countries that wish to be regarded as "developed." Objections that this arms traffic is sowing future conflict rather than peace are brushed aside. Plant 4 tells the story.

By 1950, when the Korean War began, Fort Worth was making the six-engine B-36, a prop-driven bomber that carried nuclear bombs for the Strategic Air Command (SAC). Plant 4's workforce surged to the levels of World War II, then slumped sharply a few years later when the B-52 came along with jet engines, displacing the B-36. Fort Worth moved on to the B-58 Hustler.

In the 1960s, Fort Worth peaked again on the military buildup for the Vietnam War. By then, it was manufacturing F-111s, the swing-wing fighter bomber that pounded Hanoi on many sorties over North Vietnam. (More recently, it has pounded Libya and Iraq.) The Air Force is still flying a few F-

111s, converted to electronic surveillance and jamming missions, though the plane is now marked for obsolescence.

As the United States withdrew from war in Indochina, Plant 4 suffered a severe drawdown. In the early 1970s, détente with the Russians was seriously contemplated. People expected defense cuts and a "peace dividend" devoted to domestic concerns. Fort Worth's employment fell to around seven thousand jobs. Many defense firms merged, folded, or got out of the arms business as the Pentagon budget shrank. Plant 4 did not recover until Ronald Reagan launched the buildup of the 1980s.

Fort Worth's up-and-down economic life is like a snapshot of what the Cold War years were like for most defense companies: either giddy with profit or seriously life-threatening. The boom-and-bust cycles were driven by world events or by the level of political enthusiasm for new weapons. Thus, the only meaningful competition among prime contractors has been the race to design more advanced weapons systems that will surpass the old ones made by someone else. The drive for technological perfection is inspired by the corporate fear of famine.

The Iron Triangle is a powerful fraternity, but its three sides are also in continuous struggle with one another. One firm is fat and happy with new contracts while another is starving. Politicians compete for the projects that put jobs in their districts while admirals and generals argue over which hardware should be funded for their branch. Contractors complain about the Pentagon's ham-handed procurement rules—devised by military procurement officers who have been burned by the companies' cost overruns and other forms of gouging. Incredibly tangled alliances develop among these players to advance their own aspirations.

The best of all times for Air Force Plant 4 (and for the defense industry generally) was the 1980s. The country was not at war, but it was remobilizing and modernizing armaments nonetheless. The Reagan arms buildup was generated in part by industry-financed propaganda, like the dubious claim by the Committee on the Present Danger that the Soviets had actually surpassed the United States in military might. Many people bought it, especially the politicians. Pentagon procurement spending virtually doubled (and contributed substantially to the huge federal deficits that followed).

Fort Worth caught the wave perfectly. The factory had begun making the new F-16 in 1978, and now it rolled out the small, sleek fighter planes in rapid abundance—nearly three thousand of them. By 1989 Plant 4's workforce of engineers, machinists, and managers reached thirty-one thousand—surpassing its peak in World War II.

Then peace broke out—big time and beyond denying. The Soviet enemy abruptly quit the field, actually broke up into pieces, and dissolved its empire. The defense industry was once again facing a harrowing downturn in government spending, production, and employment.

A new, more-encompassing wave of company mergers and consolidations followed. Something like three-fourths of the

120,000 companies that sold stuff to the Pentagon got out—either folded or shifted to other lines of business. Scores of factories, large and small, were closed or merged, and tens of millions of square feet in factories were idled or retired. The massive layoffs wiped out 40 percent of the industry jobs—something like one million assembly workers, engineers, and managers.

Plant 4's first blow came early in 1991: the Bush administration canceled the A-12 fighter that Fort Worth was going to build for the Navy. Massive layoffs followed within weeks. General Dynamics, which had operated the factory for four decades, sold its aircraft business to Lockheed in 1993. Two years later, Lockheed merged with Martin Marietta to become Lockheed Martin, the largest contractor of all.

Fort Worth is now down to eleven thousand employees, a number that continues to fall as existing orders get filled. Its workforce, however, remains above the low point in 1975, just as the U.S. defense budget is still larger today, in constant dollars, than it was in the mid-1970s. The workers and managers have been through this before. They hope, uncertainly, that this is just another lull.

Joe Stout, the plant's spokesman, explains the company strategy: "Work on the near-term stuff and fill the orders we've got. That's kind of what sustains us for the next few years until the F-22 comes into production." Lockheed Martin's new F-22 fighter will be assembled at its plant in Marietta, Georgia (also government-owned), but includes fuselage and other components manufactured at Plant 4.

57

"Then," Stout goes on, "Fort Worth is leading Lockheed Martin on the design team for the Joint Strike Fighter." The JSF is still in design competition—Boeing versus Lockheed Martin—but scheduled for mass production in 2008.

"Meanwhile," Stout adds, "we've got stuff that really goes beyond all that—stuff like the UCAV [Uninhabited Combat Air Vehicle]—because that's where the Air Force really seems to be headed." The UCAV, a remote-controlled fighter plane that is still in the visionary stage, may someday allow aerial combat by planes with no pilots.

In other words, Fort Worth is trying to cross a bridge into the future, maintaining a minimalist output that will keep it alive until the new projects arrive, just as it has done many times before since World War II. The newly consolidated defense industry is pursuing the same basic strategy: counting on an upturn in procurement while it promotes dazzling weapons of the future, from UCAVs to the Strategic Defense Initiative (SDI, or "Star Wars"), with alluring ads in the trade press, not to mention heavy lobbying.

"Sounds funny, but the truth of the matter is that we now are approaching the bottom," Lockheed Martin's CEO, Norman Augustine, told a business publication in 1997. "Spending will probably have to increase if America is to maintain any kind of military force at all, and there's a growing awareness of this in the Congress and the Administration. We've tried very hard to build a strong market position so that when the defense budget does turn back up, we'll be able to participate in that turnaround."

No one in the companies imagines that another Reagan boom is coming back anytime soon or that World War III is just around the corner. But neither do they expect that the military-industrial complex will be phased out.

So is this just another temporary downdraft in the life of the weapons makers? Or is the country finally confronting the over-sized defense industrial base it created half a century ago and breaking up the political-corporate-military marriage? Once you know some of the history, the answers are not so obvious.

◄o►

The vastness inside Plant 4 feels spooky at first, since acres and acres of it are cast in idle gloom. The regular columns of steel girders that I saw in the old World War II photographs are now painted bright blue, only there's not much in between them, neither workers nor machines. We're riding through the western end of the plant, where the body parts used to be fabricated for the F-16. Joe Stout is driving the electric cart down the center aisle of the mile-long plant.

The factory has 4.9 million square feet under its roof, but a quarter or more of that space is utterly empty now, reduced to bare concrete flooring. Worn white lines on the floor designate where the assembly traffic used to flow. Between the columns, each empty bay remains dimly lit, as though someone left on a night-light for the next generation of defense workers.

In the cost-cutting pressures of the defense build-down, the company has outsourced much of the fabrication work to lower-cost independent suppliers. In one bay, there's a complicated contraption overhead, a chain-link conveyor belt that used to carry finished parts to the paint shop. It's no longer used, since demand for the yellow-painted parts has fallen so drastically. Some of the huge machine tools, like a drop-hammer press that stamps aluminum sheets into pieces of fuselage, have been around since World War II. Many are stilled. Others have been outsourced, along with the jobs.

"A lot of the people who lost jobs here have gone to work in the small shops, though, of course, they're paid less money," Stout is explaining.

Further on, we begin to see a little action. A yellow crane is lifting the aft section of a fighter plane and carrying it forward to the next station. Nearby, a robot drills holes for fasteners in the skin covering for a horizontal tail fin. The F-16, Stout notes, pulls "nine Gs" at top speed; tens of thousands of fasteners keep it from ripping apart.

A few workers are moving around, too, operating the machines or finishing off the details. Despite automation, constructing the finest aircraft is still handwork at the final assembly stage. As Stout motors along the line, from the aft section to the center and forward sections, it's a real kick to watch an F-16 gradually take shape, like watching grown-up kids put together the pieces of a life-sized model airplane, only this one will fly six hundred miles an hour and fire Advanced Medium Range Air-to-Air Missiles (AMRAAM) at the bad guys.

At each assembly station, management has posted "long-range manpower projection" charts that tell workers exactly where they stand—if no new orders come in for the F-16. The board for the aft section team shows eighty-one people working now, going up briefly to eighty-five early next year, then plunging. The aft assembly team will drop to seventy-two workers by the end of 1998, then fifty-two in the second quarter of 1999, then down to thirty.

This candor may actually help morale. The assembly workers know their own seniority status in the machinists' union, so they can look at the manning projections and figure out exactly when their layoff is coming. It's probably better than not knowing.

"I'm nervous, currently," says Howard Story, an inspector on the forward section team. "Unless we get some new orders, I'm out of here in June-July 1998. And I don't see getting back in here until 2005 or 2006. That would be with the JSF, provided it gets the money from Congress. As it stands, there's no more orders on the book for the F-16. There's prospects out there. But even if we get orders today, we're looking at layoffs. I'm out of here, regardless."

Story is forty years old, earns nineteen dollars an hour, and knows he will easily find another job in the booming Fort Worth area, but not like the one he's losing. "You can find seven- and eight-dollar jobs all day long," he shrugs. "It's high-level jobs you can't get."

The ghostliness I felt upon first entering the plant takes on a human dimension: there are no young workers around—none.

In the nature of industry drawdowns, the oldest survive and the young get laid off first. This is less true for engineers and other nonunionized employees, but on the factory floor the younger machinists are gone.

Indeed, they may never return to work here, unless for some reason World War III suddenly looks plausible again. Forty-year-old Howard Story, for example, is one of the youngest left. He will be pushing fifty, even by his own optimistic calculations, before Fort Worth someday has enough production to rehire him.

"This plant was packed, I mean, full of people everywhere," says J. D. Stahl, general foreman for final assembly, who started eighteen years ago, when F-16 production was first "ramping up," as industry people put it. "It put me in awe."

By the late 1980s, the pace was furious. "To me, it was easier back then," Stahl insists. "You had more flexibility because, if you ran into a problem with one plane, we could slip another ahead of it and keep going. During those heydays, I think there were three occasions when we rolled nine airplanes out the door in a week. It was fun then."

Now the output is typically one or two planes a week. Fort Worth was turning out nearly three hundred F-16s annually in the best years. Now it's making only eighty or so a year, less than 30 percent of the old output.

And almost none of those planes are for defending America.

"When you go down the line," Bob Rearden, vice president for production operations, explains to me, "you don't see any

U.S. Air Force business to speak of. That's all foreign countries buying the F-16."

Sure enough, the six blue-gray fighters sitting at the final station, their cockpit canopies still covered by masking tape, are all destined for overseas buyers—four of them to Taiwan, two to Greece. Fort Worth still gets a handful of U.S. orders now and then, three or four planes tucked into defense appropriations bills by friendly congressmen. These are meant to replace the planes lost to attrition—the F-16s lost in crashes. But the American market for this plane is essentially over. Plant 4 is staying alive by selling its output to the rest of the world.

"In the near term," Rearden says, "I'm more concerned about what happens to our foreign sales because I don't anticipate we're going to see large manufacturing activity in this plant until the JSF."

That is, not until 2008 at the earliest. For most of the coming decade, Fort Worth hopes to keep the factory "warm" by selling as many F-16s to foreign military forces as the U.S. government will permit. The planes go to long-established allies in Europe and the Middle East, but Lockheed Martin and rival firms are constantly pushing Washington to broaden the list of eligible buyers, from Asia and Latin America to Eastern Europe.

As a business strategy, this might just succeed in getting Fort Worth across the bridge. Over the years, nearly fifteen hundred F-16s have been sold abroad to NATO nations and beyond—Israel, South Korea, Egypt, Thailand, Singapore, and Indonesia, to name a few. Selling military aircraft abroad is usually greased by deals to share some of the jobs and technology with the foreign buyer. As a result, F-16s are now also assembled in factories in South Korea, Turkey, and Belgium.

The company has a backlog of 339 planes on its overseas order book, and it expects to sell another 400–800 F-16s abroad, spread across the next ten years. That's not enough to restore robust production rates at Plant 4, but it might hold things together until something bigger comes along. If Lockheed Martin reaches its sales goal, it will wind up selling as many F-16s to foreign nations as it delivered to the U.S. Air Force.

As corporate strategy, running the production at very low levels is a sound business practice for one reason: foreign sales are exceptionally profitable for defense companies. The producers typically bump up the price for a foreign buyer, especially for developing countries anxious for the prestige of owning America's premier fighter. "The price is a political price, not a market price," one defense authority explained to me.

Furthermore, the heaviest costs of producing an F-16—the early research and development, the final design and production engineering—have already been paid for. Those costs were picked up by the original customer, the U.S. government.

"Every F-16 they sell abroad is pure gravy," says William W. Keller, a scholarly authority on multinational commerce and author of *Arm in Arm: The Political Economy of the Global Arms Trade.* "The U.S. is never going to buy more F-16s, but the sunk costs are already there, the research, the factory. That's already been covered. Now all the company has to pay for is labor, parts, and materials. Even if they only sell a few planes every year, as return on investment, it's almost pure profit."

Question: Why does the U.S. government provide a factory—rent-free—to a private firm that is manufacturing weapons purely for export and private profit? During the Cold War, defense firms could brush aside that issue with an easy answer. If the Pentagon were to charge rent for Air Force Plant 4 (or other government-owned installations), the contractor would simply add that rental cost to the price for new planes. Since weapons are procured on cost-plus contracts, the government would end up paying anyway.

Now the situation is reversed: the U.S. government is directly subsidizing new weapons for the foreign buyers because it is still picking up overhead costs of production. And it's letting the arms producers ride free on the past. The Pentagon, according to Fort Worth managers, has recently started discussing this anomaly, suggesting that a rental lease might be negotiated for the factory. The company is not enthused.

No one, however, is suggesting that Air Force Plant 4 be genuinely privatized. The taxpayers could simply sell it to Lockheed Martin (or any other willing buyer), but, of course, that's unthinkable to the Air Force. It wants to keep the Fort Worth factory under its supervision—and "warm"—because it expects to make new models there someday.

Nor is this alternative on Lockheed Martin's agenda, though the company is a vigorous advocate of privatization in other realms of government. To boost revenues, Lockheed Martin wants to take over many public functions and run them under contract, from operating military depots to managing local welfare offices. The military-industrial complex that links this private sector to government may be a troubled marriage these days, but nobody is asking for a divorce.

The largest burden of keeping Plant 4 alive lies in the inescapable overhead costs of maintaining so much unused productive capacity. As in any other business, the overhead costs get expressed in the product price. The more inefficient the factory is, the more its overcapacity raises the price for the customer. An empty factory drives up the price of everything else a company makes.

The defense-industry consultant Bob Paulson, who has advised many leading firms, including Lockheed Martin, illustrates the impact of overcapacity with the example of a nondefense business—commercial air travel. "Picture if all the airlines were forced to fly all their planes with two out of every three seats always going empty," Paulson says. "Every passenger's ticket would cost a lot more as a result. Then imagine that Congress would not let any of the airlines cancel any of their flights. That's essentially what Congress does with the defense industry."

After the Cold War, as the rate of production has gradually slowed at Fort Worth, the price of each F-16 has risen inexorably—from $20.9 million in 1990 to $42.5 million in 1997, measured in constant dollars. Even though the Air Force is buying very few planes each year, the taxpayers pick up the tab, one way or the other, for operating overhead of this basic asset. After all, it's their factory.

The managers at Fort Worth have, in fact, labored to reduce their production costs with outsourcing and "lean manufacturing" reforms, but these savings get overwhelmed in the final price by the much larger impact of the underutilized factory. Every item of cost, from heat and lighting to security guards, from management and engineers to maintenance and repair, now gets assigned to a much smaller base of output.

This price escalation is expressed in the full "program costs" to the government, costs that, in fairness to Fort Worth, also include the Pentagon's own overhead costs as the ultimate manager. The company insists that the program-cost measure is not "meaningful." It prefers to focus on the "fly-away" cost at the factory door, which is only $24 million per plane (though rising, too, with various add-ons). The trouble is, $42 million is what it truly costs the taxpayers to acquire a new F-16.

The point is not to pick on the F-16 or its producers at Fort Worth. This rising curve of prices is general across the defense industry now, the natural consequence of maintaining so much "warm" production in the post–Cold War lull. The consolidation industry has cut a lot, particularly in personnel, but it has not yet cut enough to reverse the curve. Buying fewer weapons systems, the government pays much more for each one.

The cost of all combat aircraft increased, on average, from $39 million each in 1989 to $64.5 million in 1997. The effective average price of an air-launched missile rose from $190,000 in 1989 to $314,000 in 1995. The average cost of ships rose from $325 million each to $450 million. These increases are calculated from the deliveries and program costs reported each year by the Congressional Budget Office (CBO). A few weapons systems, like the AMRAAM air-to-air missile and the C-17 transport, went the other way, but the general trend is sharply up, driven by the overcapacity. It's like a hidden inflation of peace.

"The most costly element of the defense industry process is the overhead," Bob Paulson explains. "In most defense products, the direct labor—someone who physically touches the product being made, assembles it, or writes software codes—is typically no more than half of the total product cost. That shouldn't be too surprising. We used to make hundreds of airplanes every year. Now we're making five or ten. Yet you still need a complete set of design engineers and procurement managers and accountants and lawyers and security guards, and I can go on."

During the Cold War, the concept of always maintaining underused defense factories and engineering teams—just in case—was ostensibly justified by national security. That rationale seems quite lame today, when no one can identify any rival industrial power as a serious enemy. Iraq may be dangerous, but it cannot manufacture a modern fighter plane. Some hawks nominate China as a future adversary, but if so, why are America's leading aerospace and electronics manufacturers helping China build a modern industrial base?

Of course, there was always another reason to maintain so much idle capacity in the defense industry: politics. Defense contracts enable senators and representatives to play a direct role in job creation back home, and they are naturally hostile to firms that want to close the plants where *their* constituents work. And industry managers are most reluctant to offend the congressional delegations that support their projects.

Congress, as Paulson observes, wants to have it both ways: keep the factories open but keep the costs down, even though sales and production are falling. "One of my industry clients," he says, "refers to Congress as 'the self-licking ice cream cone.'"

Put aside questions of blame. The slow-running production lines in the defense industry not only drive up the prices of new weapons but stimulate the political-corporate-military hunger for new weapons systems—new projects that will get the factories running "hot" again and able to rehire the workers who were laid off.

Crossing the bridge to the twenty-first century gets very, very expensive for the buyer.

◄○►

On the factory floor, the assembly workers naturally do not look at the F-16 this way. It has been their livelihood for many years, and they're proud of what they built for the country.

69

"This has been a real good little airplane," J. D. Stahl says. "It's been good for me and my family and for my community."

"The public has not yet got its eye on the F-22," concedes Charlie Vine, a fifty-seven-year-old coworker of Stahl's. "They say, yeah, it's expensive. Well, nowadays everything's expensive. But if you don't keep up, you're behind. We need this airplane. Hopefully, the public will see that. Not just because we're here to build it. My grandchildren will need it."

Perhaps because he is younger, Howard Story is not quite so confident of the future. "We realize we're trying to cross a bridge and the bridge is going to get slimmer," Story says. "We're just hoping we're the ones get across."

CHAPTER FIVE

"CASHING IN, CASHING OUT"

W HEN PEACE ARRIVED, THE SWORDS WERE NOT BEATEN INTO PLOWSHARES, AS THE PROPHET ISAIAH ENVISIONED. THE SWORDS, ONE MIGHT say, were beaten into capital gains. A "peace dividend" did appear after the Cold War ended. It was distributed to shareholders of the major defense companies.

When the Berlin Wall fell in 1989, a veritable storm of consolidations unfolded in the defense sector—dozens of mergers and corporate takeovers among the largest firms, deals that collectively involved more than $75 billion in capital. As a story of business strategy, it was brilliant: the defense budget shrank, yet stock prices for the major arms manufacturers soared.

The first to grasp this potential was probably Bernard L. Schwartz, CEO of Loral, then a medium-sized electronics company that supplied various elements for missiles, satellites, and other systems. Schwartz, at seventy-two, had long been an odd duck in the defense business—a liberal Democrat who grew up in Brooklyn (and had opposed the war in Vietnam), while most industry executives identified with the Republican culture of southern California. He came out of Wall Street, however, with an astute sense of what excites financial investors.

When Schwartz bought Loral in 1972, its market value was
$7.5 million. When he finally sold the defense side of the com-
pany to Lockheed Martin in early 1996 (and kept the much
smaller commercial satellite business), he estimated Loral's combined value at $15 billion. That's growth of nearly two thousand
times over. Schwartz personally owned 5 percent.

Schwartz went against the conventional wisdom on a grand
scale. The Reagan defense boom had already peaked by 1986,
and the rate of new orders was falling, though the companies
were flush with an enormous backlog of contracts that would
keep them busy for years. Defense stock prices declined as
investors recognized the threat to future earnings.

Yet Bernard Schwartz started buying. In 1987 Loral picked up
Goodyear's aerospace division, then a year or so later it acquired
the defense elements of Honeywell, Fairchild, and Ford, in rapid
succession. By 1991, as the defense cuts grew steadily larger, Loral
was buying LTV's missile business, then IBM's Federal Systems
and Unisys defense division, among others.

Stock market analysts frowned at first and knocked down
Loral's share price, but the company's revenue and earnings kept
growing with each new deal. Wall Street cheerfully got on board.

Expanding in a declining market requires nerve and vision.
What did Bernard Schwartz see ahead of the others?

First, he recognized that the fat and happy days when arms
companies were rewarded for larding more and more costs into
their production were about to end. The Pentagon would soon

be shopping desperately for savings. "These defense operations were in the hands of very large conglomerates that could not run them as efficiently as they would be in Loral's environment," Schwartz explains. "We could liberate those businesses and focus on what they knew how to do."

Schwartz also concentrated Loral's expansion on tactical weapons systems, figuring correctly that the deepest budget cuts would hit strategic weapons like the long-range nuclear missiles aimed at the Soviet Union. His acquisitions married different elements of the same systems. "At one time, we only made the sensor equipment that put the 'smart' on a smart missile," he recalls. "Then we took on building the missiles, too."

"We never bought a company doing exactly what we were doing," he explains. "If we put together vertical integration within a tactical system, we could make the front end and the back end. We could get a bigger portion of the defense budget and we could present the customer with savings. So we grew even though our market was shrinking."

Second, Schwartz assumed the government was not going to get out of arms buying. "We were not in the buggy whip business," he says. "If you're making buggy whips, you can restructure and downsize and improve efficiency, but eventually your business is going to zero. We were convinced that the shrinking pie would not be shrinking forever, that it would eventually level out and maybe even grow again."

73

As Wall Street brokers warmed to the possibilities, other firms began to play, too. General Dynamics went in the opposite direction from Loral: it sold off missile, aircraft, and other product lines to competitors like Hughes and Lockheed, then bought Bath Iron Works in Maine and consolidated around its core lines of business: subs, ships, and tanks. GD's stock, trading in the low thirties in mid-1992, was above fifty six months later.

These transactions boosted market value for both the buyers and the sellers: the buyer eliminated a competitor and shut down redundant factories and design teams; the seller cleaned up his balance sheet by dumping a losing venture and its overhead. Professor Michael Oden of Rutgers dubbed the corporate play "cashing in, cashing out."

Various scholars like Oden, community leaders, and economic development experts have devoted exhaustive study to the potential for converting America's defense manufacturing to nonlethal commercial products. A lot of conversion has occurred, and Hughes was a pioneer among the larger firms, but it was mainly done by smaller suppliers recognizing that they could no longer stay alive on Pentagon contracts. Conversion was not what the industry leaders or Wall Street had in mind.

Defense contractors had experimented with conversion back in the downdraft of the 1970s—making everything from canoes to buses to railway cars—and found it grossly unprofitable. As a Grumman executive once told George Wilson, the defense reporter for the *Washington Post,* you've got to sell an awful lot of canoes to make up for one F-14.

On Wall Street, the defense mergers were called "pure play" deals because they stuck to the arms business—and went straight to the bottom line. Wolfgang Demisch, a leading defense analyst at Bankers Trust Securities, walks me through the market's calculation in the early 1990s: "In a case like General Dynamics, they have a bunch of businesses, like the submarines and tanks, which have five or six years of market ahead in contracts to fulfill, and because these products are mature, they should be fairly profitable (if a company shrinks overhead costs). The stock market could assume that, even if at the end of this period the companies dry up and blow away, we'll still get our money back and then some." In other words, the taxpayers have already made the investment in developing the weapons—keeping them in production is very profitable for companies.

For the buyers, the acquisition is a chance to dominate a market segment and dump lots of expensive employees. "The punch line in manufacturing weapons," Demisch explains, "is that the cost is the people—engineers, accountants, salesmen and marketing people, auditors, lawyers. If you want to save some money, you eliminate the people. So a company buys two assembly lines that make the same weapon, each with its own overhead, and then it eliminates the overhead for one. This reduces the overhead costs for production from both lines."

75

In sum, the nifty arithmetic of "pure play" was: fill the back orders for weapons at the old price while drastically shrinking overhead costs. Thus, a firm's earnings per sale go up even though its sales volume is falling. And it worked: average earnings per share at nine major arms companies rose from $27 in 1989 to $40 in 1994. Once the stock market understood the logic, share prices took off, too. Lockheed Martin went up 48 percent, Northrop 50 percent, and McDonnell Douglas 80 percent.

In a sense, the companies were creaming the old contracts, squeezing an extra dollop of profit from the backlog of orders created by the Reagan arms buildup long after the Gipper had retired. A cynic might call this a corporate variation on the old "neutron bomb" approach to nuclear war: eliminate the people, keep the companies standing.

"The guys who paid the bill most severely," Wolfgang Demisch acknowledges, "were all the guys who lost their jobs, and Congress did almost nothing for them. That was a painful cost that Congress externalized. They were declared redundant, trashed, whatever you want to call it."

At the peak of the Reagan boom in the mid-1980s, 3.6 million people worked in the private defense sector. Employment is now about 2 million and still falling. Probably two-thirds of this shrinkage occurred after the Soviet collapse.

A suspicion lingers among some industry people that Washington implicitly decided to let the companies do the dirty work while politicians kept a safe distance. "My cynical view," says

Bob Paulson, "is that someone in government realized what was coming and decided: let the companies eliminate the jobs, not the Congress. That way, Congress, you won't get blamed. You can even get up and denounce the greedy defense companies that are laying off people in your district."

The Clinton administration did indeed bless the process and encourage it. In the spring of 1993, Deputy Defense Secretary William Perry, an old industry hand himself, hosted a private dinner for leading prime contractors where he predicted that half of them would probably be gone within five years. Norm Augustine of Martin Marietta, with his penchant for melodramatic metaphors, dubbed the occasion "the last supper."

But Perry was actually delivering some good news to the companies: if they proceeded with a market-driven consolidation, he told them, the Pentagon would reward them by sharing the benefits with their companies. Wolfgang Demisch explains: "Under defense contracting, if you put two companies together and you rationalize the production costs, the cost savings would normally go more or less 100 percent to Uncle Sam. That doesn't give managers and shareholders much incentive to eat the dirt. What Perry did was to say that, as long as Uncle Sam saves more on contracts, some of the cost savings could go to the companies."

This new approach was explicitly ratified a month or so later in new procurement regulations: if companies reduced costs by restructuring and consolidating, the Pentagon would let them collect a share of the future savings up-front by charging the

77

restructuring to their existing contracts. The firms began filing claims for hundreds of millions of dollars in reimbursements, a practice that will reach many billions if it's allowed to continue. When Congress finally figured out what was going on, critics denounced this reform as "payoffs for layoffs." It looks like a discreet subsidy for dumping jobs, and it is.

But does the Pentagon actually save any money? Various studies of particular weapons programs claim that, for every dollar paid to the companies, the taxpayers would save nearly two dollars or more. The trouble is, given the complexities of procurement and the fact that the per-unit costs of most weapons are rising sharply, not falling, this claim is impossible to verify. The General Accounting Office made positive savings estimates for five programs but could not identify hard proof for any of them.

"Unfortunately," the GAO defense analyst David E. Cooper testified, "what we do not have is a good number about the reductions in DOD contract prices. Real savings, if there are any, will come in the form of reduced contract prices, and we're still waiting to see those results."

Joel Johnson, vice president of the Aerospace Industries Association, has a crisp reply for the critics: "When politicians complain about payoffs for layoffs, I say, what did you expect, guys? You cut our business in half. What did you think was going to happen?"

But why should the government worry about boosting the defense companies' bottom line? "We have to reward our shareholders in the same fashion as any other industry, or we won't have shareholders," Johnson says. "We have to reward our executives in the same fashion, or we lose them." Defense CEOs collected gorgeous, multimillion-dollar bonuses for their brilliant footwork.

Since 1993, encouraged by the Pentagon, the consolidations have accelerated in speed and size. In early 1995, Lockheed and Martin Marietta merged to become "LockMartin," as industry shorthand calls this new powerhouse. Boeing picked up defense pieces from Rockwell, Litton, and others and then in 1997 took the big bite ($13.3 billion) by swallowing its only U.S. aircraft rival, McDonnell Douglas, to become "McBoeing." Hughes Electronics, owned by General Motors, bought General Dynamics' missile division, the Magnavox defense division, and others, while Raytheon acquired Texas Instruments' defense division and assorted others. Then Raytheon bought Hughes from GM for $9.5 billion.

But LockMartin still stayed ahead in the consolidation derby. In early 1996, it bought Bernard Schwartz's Loral for $9.5 billion and a year later attempted to nab Northrop Grumman for $8.3 billion. The newly enlarged company would have a significant piece of virtually every weapons system except perhaps tanks (though Northrop makes the vehicular intercommunications system for tanks).

LockMartin, with Northrop, would hold a piece of bombers (the B-2), fighters (the F-16, Navy F-18, and soon the F-22), and air transports (both the C-17 and C-130). It provides the Aegis electronics system for destroyers and cruisers, the ballistic missiles for Trident submarines, and short- and medium-range tactical missiles, air-to-air, ground-based, and sea-based. It makes the radar and missiles for Apache and Commanche helicopters. It coproduces the new Patriot III missile and various military and commercial satellites.

The result would be a company with $22 billion in arms sales worldwide, followed by McBoeing with $15 billion and Ray-Hughes (also sometimes called HughesRay) with $11 billion, according to the 1996 sales rankings by *Defense News*. United Technologies, which makes Pratt & Whitney jet engines, is a distant fourth with $3.4 billion in sales; General Dynamics, the ship and submarine maker, is fifth with $3.3 billion. A decade ago, fifteen leading contractors accounted for two-thirds of the Pentagon's spending on weapons. By 1995 the list was down to eight. Now there are three.

As he watched the action, Bernard Schwartz became increasingly scornful. He saw most of the other mergers as different from his own moves—essentially balance-sheet transactions designed to produce a punch-up for earnings and stock prices rather than genuine improvements in long-term productive efficiency.

"When you put two companies together, you can close down overhead in the corporate management—lawyers, engineers, and so forth—so you get a one-shot pickup in earnings," Schwartz explains. "You announce a restructuring with a big write-off that will boost earnings later. Companies do that over and over again and are always rewarded by the stock market. It's a sickness of Wall Street. . . . American industry pays more attention to closing plants than to building up their plants and people with new capability."

But if Loral was so successful at building up its scale and efficiency, why did Schwartz sell? Because he heard the stampede of bigger elephants bearing down on his company.

"When Lockheed and Martin Marietta merged, it was a clear signal to me," Schwartz says. "Their next objective was going to be to integrate the industry vertically [by acquiring the second and third tiers of suppliers], and this would make it increasingly difficult for other companies—even companies as large as Loral—to compete. I thought it made sense to get out." Northrop, stuck in a similar position, eventually decided to fold its hand, too.

Having bought at the bottom, Schwartz got out at the top. The sale price for Loral proved to be the peak price in the wave of takeovers: the equivalent of $1.50 for every dollar of the company's defense revenues.

After the fact, however, Schwartz saw an ominous potential in vertical integration: a prime contractor that incorporates many subsidiary elements of a weapons systems inside its own company could turn "predatory" and "eat up the subcontractors." That could squeeze out the innovation and imagination often located in the smaller independent firms.

"I think there's a danger of shrinking to just a few prime contractors," he warns. "If you have only Boeing and only Lockheed Martin [making aircraft, for instance], and they are both vertically integrated, I think it would be dangerous for the country. Many of us have been warning that if DOD allows the primes to eliminate diversity in the second or third tiers, it will be costly to the government. That battle is being fought now."

The Pentagon, having blessed the creation of "soup to nuts" prime contractors, belatedly had second thoughts of its own. A study it commissioned in 1996 by the Defense Science Board warns: "Gaining new internal sources of supply may cause a parent firm to favor the internal source over external suppliers, even if external suppliers are superior. This can not only weaken supplier-level competition but result in inferior defense products."

The Pentagon finally put its foot down. In the spring of 1998, it joined Justice Department antitrust lawyers in filing formal objections to the Lockheed-Northrop merger, arguing that it would undermine any remnant of competition in defense electronics. The two companies between them maintain six major defense aircraft works—all of them running far below capacity and in need of new orders.

The companies were shocked by the government's objections and tried to negotiate a way out of the antitrust suit. After two months, LockMartin abandoned the merger. Despite its brave talk, Northrop is left in a very precarious position for the future, reduced to second-tier status and trying to stay in the game with the three big boys.

The U.S. government's problem will not go away, however. Thanks to the consolidation it encouraged, the Pentagon is now effectively married to an oligopoly of three mammoth corporations and obliged to keep them in good health—even more visibly than it did for weak firms during the Cold War lulls. By downsizing in this manner, the military-industrial complex may now be treated, like certain major banks, as "too big to fail."

In fact, the industry-government marriage is quite incestuous because the three giants are already tightly interwoven in various production partnerships, either as prime contractors or major sub-contractors. The takeovers of second-rank firms like McDonnell Douglas, Loral, and others dramatically deepened these relationships. After all, that was the central idea behind Wall Street's "pure play" acquisitions. Everyone benefited from those transactions, except perhaps the customer.

McBoeing, LockMartin, and RayHughes will collaborate on dozens of major weapons systems. Ray Hughes and LockMartin are co-owners of the United Missile Defense Company, which builds the Patriot III. When Lockheed bought General Dynamics' production at Air Force Plant 4 in Fort Worth, its share of the F-22 airframe manufacturing went from 33 percent to 66 percent. But the other 33 percent of the F-22 belongs to Boeing. Raytheon makes the radar. On myriad other projects, one company supplies main components for another's prime contract in dizzy patterns of symbiosis.

Thus, as a matter of politics, the three big boys are already united in a cooperative competition that boils down to this: if one wins, all win. The cost-saving efficiencies promised by the corporate consolidations are quite remote in these circumstances.

How exactly are these three elephants expected to compete when they are already so closely interlocked in production? Robert Trice, Lockheed Martin's vice president for international business, insists they will, despite appearances. "You may well find the competing teams within each of those corporations," Trice suggests. "What will happen is that considerable competition will be maintained at the program level."

Others are not so optimistic. The hallmark of a market oligopoly shared among a few very large firms is their mutual interest in not disrupting things by competing too fiercely—either for market share or for lower prices.

"The behavior of the CEOs will remain absolutely focused on pleasing the customer," the consultant Bob Paulson predicts. "They will compete less aggressively because they know the government doesn't want to go down to only one company. That will lead to alternating program awards—you take this one, he gets the next one. They will be more conservative, but not necessarily more powerful."

Their awesome power may, in fact, become dependency. The bloom is already fading on defense stocks, though share prices remain far higher than five years ago. Wolfgang Demisch, for one, sees problems ahead if military spending does not revive smartly. The companies can't keep boosting stock prices by doing more takeovers since there's nothing much left to take over.

"The surviving companies are few enough that they can probably eke out a modest existence," Demisch estimates. "But is there much expectation of growth? I don't think so. Look at poor old Lockheed Martin. It has the leading aircraft fighter and missiles and satellites and defense electronics. You want stealth? They got stealth. You want laser-guided? They got laser-guided. This is a very, very capable company. Yet the stock is selling now at around 90, 91. . . . Lockheed Martin would be at 140 if it were consistent with the rest of the stock market."

The corporate gamble of massive consolidation is about whether the major defense companies can get through the current lull, keep their earnings up until new projects arrive, and, meanwhile, digest all the diverse parts they have swallowed. Bernard Schwartz thinks their timing is in question but believes they may make it.

"If they can survive, I think they are going to win the bet," Schwartz says. "The ability to hang on in these lean periods comes from bigness rather than littleness."

—◦—

A hard, painful economic paradox lurks beneath all the facts of these business maneuvers: the military-industrial complex is probably in an even deeper hole today in terms of its costly, idle factories—despite the massive layoffs and the blizzard of corporate consolidations. Scores of plants have been closed or merged in the last seven years. More than one million employees have been dismissed. Yet, overall, the defense industry resembles that

F-16 plant in Fort Worth with its acres of empty floor space and rising overhead costs. There's still too much of it.

A lot of excess productive capacity has been eliminated, but not nearly enough: the market for the weapons is shrinking even faster than the factory floor space. By not facing this reality, the Pentagon is pushing the hardest questions off into the future. Eventually this should set off explosive political arguments— whose factory must finally be closed for good?—and may even pit the Iron Triangle's three sides against one another.

"We have had what I think of as nameplate consolidations," Bob Paulson explains. "The logos have disappeared, but down at the factory level, the consolidation has been much slower. Within these companies, you still have too many factories, too many design groups, too many overhead staffs.

"Lockheed Martin, for instance, must have fifty different electronics factories now, making somewhat related defense products. If you asked Lockheed Martin management how many they would build if they could start from zero, they would probably say five, not fifty."

No one has a completely reliable estimate of how much over-capacity remains to be eliminated (especially the Pentagon, since it dodges the subject). Paulson, who surveyed the defense electronics sector for McKinsey and Company, figures electronics is operating at 40 percent or less of its potential output.

But that's better than aircraft or ships. For airplanes, the over-all level of output is probably more like Air Force Plant 4—

around one-third of its capacity—and some aircraft assembly lines are operating closer to zero. The government bought only seven ships this year. But there are still six major shipyards in business, waiting for Navy orders.

By comparison, a profitable commercial enterprise maintains an efficient level of output at around 85 percent of its plant capacity. Jacques S. "Jack" Gansler, an industry authority, estimated in his book *Defense Conversion* that the defense industry was producing at only 35 percent of capacity by the mid-1990s, and even this low rate "was rapidly declining even further."

The clearest evidence that he's right is the general trend of rising per-unit costs for weapons. The GAO studied six major defense firms and found that, despite mergers and downsizing, four of them still had rising overhead costs—costs that feed into their contract prices to the government.

"The point people miss," Gansler says, "is not that the defense companies are making huge profits. It's that they're charging huge costs to the government to pay for all of this excess capacity that they've got lying around. The government pays for all of that. The problem is, if a company becomes a sole-source contractor and there is no competition, then they have no incentive to reduce costs."

In other words, the consolidations accomplished much less than it appeared—at least in terms of streamlining the defense industry for an era of peace. The paradox was explained by Professor Michael Oden, who studied seventeen takeover deals and

87

found the primary motive in most cases was extending a company's market reach by acquiring new product lines rather than merging duplicate assembly lines. "The immediate cost saving achievable through these types of combinations is not obvious," Oden wrote.

Some genuine mergers of production did occur. Hughes bought General Dynamics' missile line in San Diego, shut down its own missile plant in Los Angeles, and merged both in Tucson. "Our plant utilization went from 35 percent to 85 percent," Hughes CEO Michael Armstrong told the *Los Angeles Times.* "We had significantly less cost. Our hourly bid rate went down." Lockheed Martin did something similar with its satellite manufacturing, combining three scattered factories into one new one at Sunnyvale, California.

This rationalization of the big three has only just begun. Paulson has launched a new investment banking firm, Aerostar Capital, to acquire promising business subsidiaries from the defense conglomerates—to liberate them, as Bernard Schwartz did.

But the management problem originates in politics. With a couple of exceptions, like the F-14, the Pentagon and Congress have declined to cancel *any* major weapons systems. So the assembly lines are kept intact, despite rising costs and dwindling orders. The old argument about maintaining a "warm" industrial base becomes keeping it "lukewarm."

"The most obvious interpretation of this murky process is that the DOD is more concerned with keeping capacity in weapons production than in achieving savings," Oden wrote in his 1996 paper for the Council on Foreign Relations. "In newly combined and diversified companies, high profits are allowed on production contracts in one weapons area in order to maintain the capability to carry out new development programs in another defense segment."

Thus, in order to build the F-22 or the Joint Strike Fighter someday, the Air Force tolerates gross inefficiency at the factory level now. "It's almost as if we designed all these industries to do the wrong thing," Paulson muses. "Keep all these factories going because the government is willing to pay the excess cost. Not just willing, it's *eager* to pay the cost, for all the usual political and social reasons."

It seems unlikely taxpayers can be persuaded to tolerate the burden of this costly excess, as they did for many years during the Cold War. Regardless of public opinion, however, the industry and its customer, the Pentagon, are on a collision course with their own desires.

The armed services are going to find themselves paying more and getting less, given the present trend of rising costs and the higher levels of complexity designed into future weapons. Even if defense budgets start rising again, the Air Force will still have to shrink its fighting force significantly because it will be paying much more for each new airplane and therefore buying fewer of them.

The spiraling prices ahead were described by Gansler, who was vice president of TASC (The Applied Science Corporation), which advises defense companies and the Pentagon: "The cost per plane will rise two to one over past decades as this process continues." The same warning is sounded by the Defense Science Board, which Gansler formerly chaired, in a recent procurement study: "If one looks at the number of aircraft per unit dollar in the past and the number per unit dollar in the future, one can see that in the past the DOD got twice as many aircraft for the same number of dollars."

The inexorable logic of this trend has not as yet deflected the Pentagon or the industry from their visions of spectacular new weapons for the future (though the budget squeeze did force cutbacks in the projected buy orders, a step that automatically pushes the per-unit costs even higher). The collision that lies ahead will probably pit one factory against another, one congressional delegation against another. It may also pit defense companies against some of their favorite members of Congress.

Northrop Grumman, as an aircraft manufacturer that also supplies major components for other producers, seems especially vulnerable to the squeeze that's coming. Its rival for future projects may be the company that wanted to swallow it—Lockheed Martin. Northrop operates three aircraft assembly plants for fighters and bombers; Lockheed has three itself. For political reasons, it is already spreading F-22 production between Fort Worth and the Marietta, Georgia, factory though either plant could easily produce the whole aircraft. When there is no longer enough work to go around, the Pentagon may have to cut out Northrop rather than damage its primary producer.

But will LockMartin get enough new orders for future projects to keep *all* of its aircraft factories running? If not, which factories does it intend to close? Or will it try to keep all of them going to appease the congressional patrons?

If so, the burdensome overhead costs will have to be pushed off onto someone else, presumably the taxpayers. Bob Paulson describes the dilemma: "The CEO at Lockheed Martin needs to build a new fighter plane. He's got all of these factories, and none of them is full. So where does he put the work? Ideally, ignoring the politics, the CEO would like to put all of the work in one or two of those factories and close the others so that, over time, he will wind up with 70–80 percent utilization and save a lot of money.

"But that requires him to tell at least half of the congressmen who are supporting him: 'I'm closing the plant in your district. I'm laying off all those loyal workers who used to applaud your speech at the ceremony where we roll out the new plane, workers who have always voted for you and contributed to your campaign.' Defense contractors are very loyal to Congress. They would never embarrass a congressman who supports them because the people who give out the contracts can also take them away."

Yet, if LockMartin and the Air Force don't start taking such steps, they are going to be embarrassed by the escalating costs of their new weapons. This is not a theoretical dilemma. A series of threatening choices is bearing down on the military-industrial complex.

"Someday soon," Paulson predicts, "when the F-22 goes to full production, Lockheed Martin will have to put the bulk of the work in one place or the other. That means they've got to tell one of those delegations—Texas or Georgia—the bad news pretty soon."

If LockMartin does find a way to keep both Texas and Georgia happy, the rest of the country must find a way to pay for it.

—◄o►—

Jack Gansler is a comfortable member of the fraternity but also an amiable crusader for reform. During the post-Vietnam lull of the 1970s, while serving as an assistant Defense secretary, Gansler recognized the extraordinary costs of keeping so many idle factories in place, ready for war. He began proselytizing for a fundamental conversion of the military-industrial complex, starting with the bloated aircraft sector.

America, he argued, should move away from maintaining this singular industrial sector devoted to manufacturing weapons. Instead, companies should be prodded into merging their commercial-military production—dual-use assembly lines that could switch back and forth from different products, that would be both more efficient and less dependent on the Pentagon to keep them alive.

Gansler was politely brushed aside. The industry instead was busy promoting the Soviet threat and persuading politicians to launch the huge new round of weapons buying that became the Reagan defense boom.

Twenty years later, the industry is mired in another down-draft and Gansler is back, making the same essential arguments about how to reform defense production. Only this time the company executives will at least have to listen politely because Gansler has become the new deputy Defense secretary for logistics and acquisitions, the key position to make sense of these contradictions. That means he will be speaking for the customer—urging the armed services to become smarter buyers, rewarding the companies that respond to his vision.

Given the history, Jack Gansler is remarkably optimistic that these ideas can prevail now, though he acknowledges that most companies remain unenthused. Why should they change now? "Because all the defense orders aren't going to be in enough quantity to support defense production," Gansler predicts. "So as the defense dollars shrink, the companies will have to go commercial and DOD will have to seek commercial suppliers for lots of stuff."

Some of this shift is already occurring, Gansler claims, and delivering enormous savings. Instead of designing state-of-the-art weaponry with performance standards that are extremely expensive to produce, the services are discovering they can buy some commercial components off the shelf. TRW, for instance, manufactures computer cards for the F-22 electronics on its commercial assembly line.

"The TRW people said, 'Gee, if you'd let us design this in the first place, we could have cut the cost even more, but as it is, we can only cut the cost 40 percent,'" Gansler relates.

Companies like Boeing have kept their military and commercial production separate, partly because the Pentagon procurement regulations are so cumbersome, but perhaps also because they didn't want to dilute the efficiency of their commercial assembly lines with the wasteful practices tolerated by their military customer. Nevertheless, efficient integration of the two has been achieved elsewhere, Gansler observes.

"Go to the Japanese heavy industries, and that's what you see," he explains. "Mitsubishi and the other Japanese companies make military and commercial products in the same factories."

What's most important about Gansler's idea is that it would put to rest the old World War II argument that the United States must keep paying, decade after decade, for a huge, grossly inefficient defense industrial base. These underused factories, he explains, "are maintained solely for potential surges in production in times of crisis. If an integrated base existed, this additional capacity requirement could be satisfied by temporarily shifting work from the commercial to the military area within the same facility."

In other words, if World War III should suddenly loom as a real possibility, America could do what it did in 1942, only this time it would not be flatfooted. It would have a big head start. "If reconstitution of a large defense industrial base is ever required in the future," Gansler has written, "the fact that the military equipment has been designed to be built in commercial plants will greatly facilitate the transformation."

His logic is impeccable and persuasive. Yet Jack Gansler may wind up once again an unheeded visionary, not on the economics but on the politics. To get to where Gansler wants to go, the United States would have to truly demobilize at last from the arms-making mobilization of World War II. That is, we would have to close those old factories for good—pay the cost of wiping out all that excess capacity and employment. The adjustment would be painful, for sure, but it would also liberate tens of billions for other public purposes.

Is America willing to face the peace and prepare for it? Not yet. Both the armed services and the industry are headed in the opposite direction: imagining new generations of high-tech weaponry that will get at least some factories humming again.

When I interviewed Gansler some months before he was tapped for the Pentagon job, he was envisioning a radical shift in the military's thinking. The budget squeeze, he predicted then, would force cancellation of some major projects. For the future, new weaponry can be developed and designed, but not produced in large numbers. Keep up the technology, but don't manufacture a lot of stuff you don't really need.

"The Air Force isn't going to give up on fighter planes," he said then, "so we will probably have one more new plane. But my guess is they will cancel the F-22 and go ahead with the Joint Strike Fighter because it's a cheaper plane. Then just build a few of them in the out-years." But Secretary Cohen's quadrennial defense review canceled nothing major. The Air Force still wanted both the F-22 and the JSF. Once in office, Gansler had another opportunity to defer the F-22's production, but he folded. Lockheed Martin was given half a billion to produce the first two planes, even though the F-22 was still far short of passing all the required flight-testing. The GAO had recommended that production be postponed for a year, at least until testing could be completed.

Instead, Gansler chose a fig-leaf solution: relabeling the first two aircraft "preproduction test vehicles." He claimed the Pentagon could still stop the program at a future date. Based on the history of arms procurement, that seems exceedingly unlikely.

In fact, the F-22 was threatened, not for reasons of grand defense strategy but because the airplane lost its chief sponsor in Congress: Rep. Newt Gingrich of Georgia. It was only the first act in what promised to be an intense political drama; Lockheed Martin mobilized to save the project. But Bob Paulson's prediction appears to be coming true: major procurement issues are now to be settled on the basis of regional political muscle.

The consequence of not facing these questions rationally is becoming clear even to the most bellicose politicians: The Pentagon cannot pay for it. The companies will argue otherwise and hope for an end to the lull. And the arms makers do have a fallback. If the U. S. won't buy their weapons, they will sell them to the world.

CHAPTER SIX

GOING GLOBAL

EXPANDING NATO BY ADDING THREE FORMER SOVIET SATELLITES AS ALLIANCE MEMBERS IS HAILED BY THE CLINTON WHITE HOUSE AS A GREAT diplomatic achievement. The unstated political objective, however, is to open new markets for the American arms industry. Early last spring, while the diplomats were still arguing over which nations would be invited to join, Norman Augustine was already on the ground in Poland, Hungary, the Czech Republic, Slovenia, and Romania, making the pitch for Lockheed Martin fighter planes and air transports, communications satellites, radar, and other military hardware.

"Let me be clear," Augustine told audiences of policy makers on his five-nation tour. "Lockheed Martin aspires to play a significant role in developing the infrastructure of Central Europe for the twenty-first century."

For decades, these nations had no choice in the matter: they bought their weapons from the Soviets. Now that they are joining the other team, they will be expected to adapt their military forces accordingly—that is, buy the more advanced weaponry manufactured in the triumphant West.

"We are extremely proud," the LockMartin CEO pointed out to Poles, Hungarians, and others, "that we have provided state-of-the-art systems to NATO since its inception nearly fifty years ago.

We are particularly proud that our systems—such as the F-16, the C-130, and the FPS-117 early warning radar—have become the NATO standard. Once invitations are issued at the Madrid summit, the countries of Central Europe will have to step up to tough choices on modernization of equipment and the requirement to achieve inter-operability with NATO forces."

Money is a problem, he acknowledged, since none of the new NATO members has spare wealth to devote to F-16s, but his company is already offering discount prices to win a permanent foothold in the new market. Furthermore, the Pentagon is offering new loan and credit subsidy programs that will help grease the sales.

"We believe that we can solve the problem of NATO integration most quickly, most comprehensively, and at lowest cost," Augustine promised the fledgling allies. He is listed as "senior adviser" to the U.S. Committee to Expand NATO, a promotional group formed by industry and foreign policy leaders. Its president is Bruce L. Jackson, LockMartin's director of strategic planning.

Augustine made one other commitment to the prospective buyers: Lockheed Martin will share the jobs with them. "We're serious about being a global company, and that means expanding our workforce outside the United States," Augustine declared. "We are looking at joint venture structures, potential investment opportunities, and other mechanisms to facilitate our international partnerships. We would like to become the partner of choice for European companies."

Actually, the practice of sharing production jobs and technology with the weapons buyers is a long-established feature of Cold War arms sales—encouraged by the U.S. government as a way to foster military modernization among allies. The customers demand a piece of the action, and the economic exchange helps poor countries pay for their expensive new weapons. Given America's huge drawdown in defense employment, the practice now looks like added insult to the displaced workers at home. As Augustine told Europeans, LockMartin itself combines seventeen different companies that have collectively eliminated more than one hundred thousand jobs.

Back in Washington, an industry authority puts a more cynical spin on what the NATO expansion portends: "We're going to lend them the money to buy our stuff—and some of our stuff will actually be made there."

The end of the Cold War rivalry has in fact opened a fierce new global competition among the arms makers—American, European, and Russian. They are competing now for customers that were once off limits to them, and all are struggling with the same fundamental problem of how to keep their factories going in a shrinking market. The overcapacity problems facing the U.S. industry are even more severe for Western European companies—and overwhelming for the old Soviet weapons industry.

NATO expansion is the visible expression of the arms race that is under way, not among warring nations, but among the anxious manufacturers confronted with peace. Since the end of the Cold War, the volume of international arms sales has not increased, but the U.S. share of the global market has gone up, while Russia's share has shrunk drastically. LockMartin's overseas business, for instance, went from 5 percent to 18 percent of its total sales in just five years. Central Europe offers a market of two hundred fighters over the next five years—$8 billion to $10 billion in scarce orders.

"We will certainly fight to sell aircraft to Poland and Hungary, Romania, and what not," says Joel Johnson of the Aerospace Industries Association. "Everybody and his uncle wants to do that. These countries aren't going to increase their defense spending, but they want to shift from Russian to Western suppliers. If there's any rationale for NATO, it is that we want them to have compatibility with our weapons."

Poland's air force, for instance, consists of 437 Soviet-made combat aircraft, and it wants to replace 100 of them. But should it buy F-16s from Lockheed Martin or F-18s from Boeing? The French Mirage or the JAS-39 from Saab and British Aerospace? All are competing for the sale; even Russia is offering Poland bargain-priced MIG-29s. LockMartin is proposing an industrial "partnership" to help Poland offset its costs. The U.S. Air Force, meanwhile, is offering to set up aerospace management centers in Central Europe. The Navy has suggested leasing some of its F-18s to Poland.

The Pentagon and the industry, in other words, are jointly promoting American-made weapons, and with considerable success. In 1995 U.S. producers delivered $12.5 billion in weapons to foreign buyers, three-fourths of them destined for developing nations. The U.S. volume represents 44 percent of the global market, more than double America's market share in 1990 when the Soviet Union was the leading exporter of arms. Now Russia is a weak third, behind Great Britain.

America's head start in selling arms to the new NATO members helps explain why the other major allies are unenthused about paying for the alliance's expansion—a burden variously estimated from $27 billion to $125 billion. France's President Jacques Chirac has said that France will not devote a single franc more to the enterprise. Now that the Cold War is over, Chirac observed, "I don't know why the defense of the alliance should cost more than it did then." German Chancellor Helmut Kohl complained that "it is completely absurd to link NATO enlargement with cost factors as if the aim is to rearm large areas of Europe to the teeth." Both Kohl and Chirac have made unsubtle suggestions that the American motive for expanding NATO is selling weapons.

In fact, the allies are competing head to head for these sales. "Those countries like the Czech Republic want to distance themselves as far away from the Russians as they can—that's a positive sales point for us," say Joel Johnson. "But the French will say to them, 'If you guys want to be European and part of our Europe, buy our stuff, not the American stuff.' That's a negative for us. But a positive is: our stuff works."

A more dangerous consequence of this new post–Cold War competition is the hard squeeze it puts on the weakened Russian industry, driving it further down the food chain of potential buyers. Losing their old market, Russian manufacturers are tempted to unload surplus weaponry on the more marginal or dangerous regimes, the so-called rogue nations, like Iraq or Algeria or North Korea, that America tries to contain with trade embargoes.

"Yes, it's a dilemma," Johnson cheerfully acknowledges. "The Russians are most likely to sell to some unpleasant people. But what are you going to do about it? The solution is not to make the Czechs buy from their former oppressors. The solution is to convince Congress to go spend some serious money on helping the Russian economy."

Diplomatic efforts to contain this trend with new arms limitations agreements that put certain nations off limits are doomed to irrelevance, Johnson believes. "If you have an arms agreement, what you're doing is taking the market away from the Russians and the Chinese," he explains. "And they say: 'What are you going to do for us in return?' The answer is: nothing, absolutely nothing. So is it any wonder that they aren't signing up? Any arms agreement would deny our competitors markets that are already closed to us."

The market squeeze on the old Soviet industrial base has a ripple effect around the world, starting with Latin America. Last year, the Republic of Belarus sold a batch of old MIG-29s and

Su-25 fighters to Peru. The question was immediately asked: If Peru can acquire advanced combat aircraft, why not Chile, Argentina, Brazil, and others? American companies seized on that transaction as the pretext for demanding that the United States allow them to sell premier fighter planes to other South American nations. In 1997 the Clinton administration lifted an informal embargo that had been in place for twenty years. Chile leads the list of prospective buyers for F-16s.

Yet the Belarus sale to Peru is a dubious precedent for launching a continental arms competition. As Richard F. Grimmett, defense specialist at the Congressional Research Service, reported, the Peruvians bought a lot of old aircraft that aren't really ready for warfare. "The Russian military complains," Grimmett says, "that its reputation is damaged because this old stuff is being sold at fire-sale prices and can't be maintained. That squadron sent to Peru is not 10 percent operational and can't be supported. This is the sale the U.S. is using to justify new sales to Chile. This is the wedge that opens the whole ball game in Latin America."

By mid-1998 the South American arms race was revving up. Saab–British Aerospace, France's Mirage, LockMartin, and McBoeing were all bidding to sell Chile up to sixteen fighters for $600 million. Chile pressed to get AMRAAM missiles for its new aircraft. Brazil's air force intended to spend between $3 billion and $4 billion buying seventy to one hundred fighters from one of the same companies, or maybe even from the Russians.

103

Defense spending by Latin American nations has increased by 35 percent since 1992, while their economies have grown by 22 percent. No one quite knows why these countries feel so threatened, but perhaps they have come to feel threatened by each other.

One obvious danger of distributing so much advanced weaponry among so many scattered nations is that someday, in unforeseeable ways, this hardware may be facing us on the battlefield. The ideological boundaries of the Cold War imposed some arbitrary limits on who could sell to whom. Without those inhibitions, the arms marketplace is becoming truly global.

As Professor William Keller describes it in *Arm in Arm*, the casual trade by Western arms producers in the Middle East laid the groundwork for Saddam Hussein's aggression and led to Desert Storm. Iraq, after all, bought its advanced weaponry from many sources, including U.S. allies like France. "The whole point of the Gulf War," Keller says, "was that we did what we had to do because of the errors we committed in the past."

Industry people respond with a shrug. They claim to be selling security and stable friendship, not future adversaries. Besides, if we don't sell stuff to Indonesia or Thailand or whomever, then somebody else will. Bob Paulson gives a concise summary of the industry rationale: "If we don't sell to them, will the French? Yes. If they buy our weapons, will we exercise more control over them? Possibly. Are we putting machine guns in the hands of some savages? Perhaps. But someone will if we don't."

Industry people further claim that it's okay to sell our older weapons like the F-16 to other countries since we will stay ahead by developing new generations of high-tech weapons systems that can still dominate anything the enemy has. The F-16 may be the best in the world for now but will soon be outgunned by the F-22, then the Joint Strike Fighter later on. Thus, the foreign proliferation of our best weapons becomes another force promoting more research and development funding for futuristic armaments.

The relaxed official view toward exporting advanced technologies for armaments got a nasty shock in 1998 when India abruptly detonated a nuclear bomb of its own. Among other reasons, India cited the fact that U.S. companies had been selling high-tech goods to China and that China had been sharing nuclear-missile technology with Pakistan (which responded to India with its own nuclear test a few weeks later).

As the facts unfolded, the political controversy landed at the doorstep of Bernard Schwartz of Loral. While he was putatively out of the defense business, his company and Hughes had won government permission—over objections from Pentagon experts—to launch commercial satellites in China. Chinese satellite launchers are cheaper, the companies argued, and the Clinton administration approved the deal in pursuit of global markets.

But the commercial venture also risked leakage of very sophisticated missile technology to the Chinese military, and critics charge that this has occurred. Whether it did or not, the transaction fed a chain of paranoia in neighboring nations and became a new rationale for nuclear proliferation. Provoking inadvertent crisis may be profitable for weapons firms, but it does not seem to be in the national interest—or, for that matter, the world's.

"Using arms exports as a way to maintain defense industrial capacity is a particularly irrational policy," Michael Oden has argued. "A Lockheed official recently testified that the U.S. has to make a multibillion-dollar commitment to the F-22 to counter the widespread proliferation of higher-performance combat aircraft such as the U.S.-made F-15 and F-16. . . . This argument suggests that, with the fall of the Soviet Union, we are effectively engaging in an arms race with ourselves."

As a matter of fact, the industry also wants to start selling the F-22 around the world right now, even before the new plane becomes operational at home. The foreign sales would help in business terms, keeping up the factory output and holding down the per-unit costs, since the Pentagon has cut back its own buy order. If European allies are allowed to buy the F-22 now, it's argued, maybe they would abandon their own plans to build the "Eurofighter" as a market competitor. Besides, Johnson assures the skeptics, "we're not talking about selling F-22s to any of those bad guys out there."

The most troubling prospect, however, is not the current pace of arms sales but the major companies' strategic plans to become globalized firms themselves—multinational producers with factories, design teams, and jobs scattered among partners across many countries. To that end, the Americans are buying stakes in foreign companies, forming corporate alliances that will share markets and production across national boundaries, eliminating excess capacity and also potential competitors. This multinational strategy has threatening implications for U.S. employment obviously, but a far greater danger may eventually confront the government itself as its control over the defense industry it originally created is weakened. A multinational firm based in many nations, with many different patrons, may find its loyalties scattered, too.

Lockheed Martin is exploring partnership with the German-French-British consortium that manufactures Airbus commercial airliners. (Airbus is the sole remaining commercial competitor with Boeing, which, remember, is itself a partner with LockMartin on many military projects.) Boeing has bought a stake in a Czech company. Lockheed Martin acquired 49 percent of Argentina's aerospace company. Textron Bell bought part of a Romanian helicopter maker. Roll-Royce bought Allison, a U.S. firm that does super–cruise missile work. Boeing and Lockheed Martin both sought British Aerospace as a major partner in the Joint Strike Fighter competition.

"LockMartin and McBoeing and RayHughes have gone as far as they can go in the U.S. consolidation," says Joel Johnson. "There will be some swapping of bits and pieces, but the logic for them now is to look offshore. If the European industry's consolidation doesn't seem to be going anywhere, there will probably be more European companies looking to hook up with the U.S. companies. It's like riding a bicycle—if you stop, you fall down because you run out of forward motion. The domestic defense market is flat, the space program is probably flat. So you're going to want to globalize."

If the arms makers do succeed in globalizing, the political implications are profound. "If the defense industrial base becomes truly international," Professor Keller warns, "then you are rupturing the relationship between the government and the industrial part of its national security apparatus. The strategy assumes that these defense firms are private companies when they are really creations of the state. Now the government is saying: 'We can't afford you guys any longer.' So the companies say, 'Okay, we're consolidating and going global. That way you can have new weapons at cheaper prices.' But the new question will be: Which government is the client? What if a government wants a company to do something that doesn't make good business sense and the company says no? What do you do if you have a company fully globalized and willing to sell weapons to anyone?"

As U.S. commercial companies have globalized their operations, their loyalties to the nation—and to the workforce back home—have steadily weakened. What Keller suggests is that the same trend is now beginning among the arms makers, but with much more dangerous potential. Imagine a military-industrial complex that is truly multinational in scope and scale and able to play governments off against each other. Imagine a global arms market that claims to be above and beyond the political control of mere nations. These prospects are only theoretical at present, but one can hear their global dreams in the hopeful expressions of the leading executives.

Norman Augustine promises: "We're serious about being a global company, and that means expanding our workforce outside the United States."

Philip Condit, chairman of Boeing, tells the *Financial Times* of London that, twenty years hence, people will think of Boeing as a global company, not an American company, and he acknowledges the national security problem that a globalized arms firm creates: "Because we are a U.S. defense contractor, our board members will have to have security clearance. As we move in an international direction, we will have to find ways—the U.S. government will have to find ways—of dealing with that."

Boeing's new head of military sales, Alan Mullaly, rhapsodizes over the corporate vision for global peace. "What's really cool about defense," Mullaly tells the *Economist*, "is that it will no longer be about defending America, but about making the world safe."

But they aren't making the world safer. By pushing more and more weaponry, old and new, on other nations, the arms manufacturers are laying the groundwork for future conflicts. No one can say when or where or identify the adversaries. But Iraq and Iran ought to have taught the advanced economies that today's ally and customer may become tomorrow's "rogue nation." If that occurs again, of course, the military-industrial complex will use the bad news to argue for renewed vigilance at home—and more advanced weapons that can trump the new enemy equipped with the old U.S.-made weapons.

◄○►

CHAPTER SEVEN

THE END OF THE LINE

IR FORCE PLANT 42 RISES FROM AN EMPTY
EXPANSE OF MOJAVE DESERT, AMID PATCHES OF
GREASEWOOD AND JOSHUA TREES, LIKE A MONU-
ment to the industrial conquest of nature. It is situated in the
Antelope Valley, a domesticated section of desert an hour or so
northeast of Los Angeles, with factories and subdivisions and a
town called Palmdale where one hundred thousand people live.
A light smog floats above the desert floor, obscuring the mountain rim. The factory at site 4 is a huge windowless building,
painted pale brown and surrounded by lots of high wire fences.

This is where Northrop Grumman manufactured, in great
secrecy, the stealthy bat-winged bomber known as the B-2, a
plane that could fly deep into the Soviet Union, eluding enemy
radar, and deliver eighty 500 pound bombs, without even
requiring a fighter-plane escort—except that the first B-2s did
not come into operational status until a year or so after the
Soviet Union ceased to exist.

Inside the government-owned plant, the vast assembly hall
looks like an empty sports arena—one million square feet of floor
space with a girdered ceiling one hundred feet overhead. "You can
fit the LA Coliseum in here, you really could," a Northrop man
volunteers, when I express awe. The floor is occupied by seven
workstations, each a complicated web of scaffolding and

machines, where bombers moved through the various stages of final assembly. Originally, the project was totally "black": employees could not even tell their families what they were working on. Elaborate screens divided the factory floor so that workers in one section could not observe what other workers were doing.

Across the far wall, a huge red-white-and-blue banner still proclaims: "America Is Counting on Us, Make It Happen!" Only, at the moment, a single aircraft sits on the shop floor, an already completed B-2, called the *Spirit of South Carolina,* that's been brought back from Whiteman Air Force Base for further upgrading and testing. The rest is idle.

Unlike the F-16 plant in Fort Worth and other defense factories that originated back in World War II, the Palmdale B-2 plant is new; built fifteen years ago, it was just hitting its prime when the Cold War ended. The original plan in 1981 called for Northrop to make 132 bombers of the new stealthy design. The factory was engineered to turn out 3 a month, 36 a year, at the peak rate. After the Berlin Wall fell in 1989, the Pentagon cut its order back to 75. Then, in early 1992, President Bush capped the B-2 production at 20 planes. At its height, the project had employed 12,500 people, the majority of them at the huge fabrication plant in Pico Rivera in southeast Los Angeles County, where composite materials were molded into the supple leading-edge contours that give the B-2 its stealthy quality.

Now the end is near. The jobs are rapidly disappearing. In the election year of 1996, Congress and President Clinton scraped together the money to pay for one additional B-2, but the workload is inevitably dwindling. Layoffs are accelerating at Pico Rivera, and its labs have been moved to other locations. It will be closed for good by 1999. Northrop is already trying to sell off the acreage and filing for lower tax assessments on its devalued factory.

The assembly workers at Palmdale, now fewer than four thousand, will have finishing chores to do on the final two bombers, but they, too, will all be gone in a couple of years. A marvelous modern industrial facility, sitting in the middle of the desert and equipped to make more stealthy bombers, is utterly redundant.

But wait, maybe not. The political side of the Iron Triangle is not yet ready to give up on the B-2. The 1997 defense authorization bill drafted in the House provided advance funding to keep the factory alive so that it could manufacture nine more B-2s. This last-gasp revival is supported by members from California, Texas, Georgia, Washington, and allied delegations loyal to the companies and workers.

Before the LockMartin takeover was cancelled, the B-2 belonged to the Big Three of defense manufacturing. Lock-Martin expected to absorb the prime contractor, Northrop. Boeing makes the B-2's center fuselage, and RayHughes makes its radar. The contractors and subcontractors united to concoct theoretical justifications for building more B-2s despite the fact that the Pentagon didn't ask for them. If the B-2 is raised from the dead, it will demonstrate the awesome political clout of those three companies when they want the same thing.

On the House floor, Representative Ron Dellums, the ranking Democrat on the National Security Committee and a longstanding critic of the bomber, argued with exasperation against the new commitment. Don't members know, he asked, that five different authoritative studies have concluded that the bomber force does not need any more B-2s? Don't they understand that the $27 billion that will be required eventually to buy these planes must come out of something else, either other weapons systems or domestic programs? Don't they realize that, even if more B-2s are ordered, the jobs are not coming back?

Dellums lost, 216–209. It seemed a hopeful victory for the bomber, its manufacturers, and workers. But when I visited Palmdale and Pico Rivera a few days after the House roll call, I was surprised that the engineers and machinists facing layoffs were not much elated. Defense workers long ago learned to live with the up-and-down nature of their industry—the giddy booms and the long, painful lulls. They were grateful for the eleventh-hour rescue effort, but most of them still assumed that the B-2 was probably finished. In any case, as Dellums had explained to his House colleagues, the workers knew their jobs weren't coming back.

"The clock is definitely ticking," Joel Mabon, a burly thirty-five-year-old forklift driver, says cheerfully. "Maybe, if Congress votes for more planes, it will tick a little slower. But everyone knows what's coming."

Larry Butgereit, a fifty-one-year-old engineer, had been hoping to retire from Northrop in two years. Now he has his 120-day layoff notice and is looking for something else. "Even if they do get House and Senate approval, it's not going to save a lot of jobs here," he say stoically. "Unless something drastic happens in the world, it's not going to save any jobs for us."

At Pico Rivera, the laid-off engineer and managers going through interviews at the job placement office were even less impressed by the congressional action. "I think it's a crying shame the program has been discontinued," says Ed McBratney, a software engineer who worked fifteen years on the B-2. "I turned the lights on over here. We started in '82, and it was pretty fascinating. We were doing things here that had never been done anywhere before. Everything was leading-edge. It felt good to be out there in the lead. When I heard about the House vote, I thought, this is great. But then I realized, what is it really going to mean for the workforce?"

"The others feel badly for me, they wish me well," says Don Young, an anxious electronics engineer in his fifties who's just been laid off. "They hope it's not going to happen to them. But believe me, it will."

A Northrop corporate spokesman, Ed Smith, more or less confirms the employees' analysis of job prospects. Whatever happens in Congress, he tells me, it won't reverse the situation for the workforce. "Not at Pico Rivera," Smith says. "At Pico, it's pretty much a done deal." At Palmdale, the company has already set employment at a maximum of thirty-five hundred. "The assembly workforce stays the same," he explains, "whether it's nine or thirty planes."

If the news seems grim, the employees at both plants are remarkably cheerful about the cloud hanging over their livelihoods. They know the score. They are not kidding themselves. Susan Andorfer, who has worked ten years in configuration management at Palmdale, says few of her colleagues have any illusions about the future. "The bottom line is: if you're not looking now, you should be," she says. "Everyone we know is looking right now."

The jobs aren't coming back. The realism of these workers is a bracing contrast with the political fancies still nurtured in Congress. As Ron Dellums tried to tell his colleagues, the days of defense production as the government's major jobs program are over—regardless. Nevertheless, the B-2's political coalition did not give up. In the Senate, where skeptics had more power, new funding for nine more bombers was rejected. But the final compromise worked out in conference committee did keep the question of the B-2's fate alive for future discussion. Advanced funding was provided for the additional bombers, but the president would not be required to spend the money.

This deal guarantees that the politics of bat-wing bombers will play out in future elections. Presidential candidates in 2000 will doubtless be asked to commit themselves to spending the money—building more B-2s. When they are campaigning in

California, Texas, Washington, and other B-2 states, they may be tempted to say yes. Who knows, maybe stealthy bombers should be kept on hand in the event that we wish to bomb China someday, or maybe India, or even Russia if the Communists come back to power. The episode demonstrates that Congress still resists making the hard, final choices that would truly shut down the Cold War.

But too many economic forces are pushing in the opposite direction. The defense industry remains mired in gross overcapacity and must undertake huge additional cutbacks if it is to achieve reasonable levels of cost efficiency. As the companies make hard choices between their existing plants, the benefits of defense spending are becoming more and more concentrated in a few states—Georgia, Texas, California. The competition for foreign sales and global partners drives the companies to move more and more of their production offshore rather than rehire idle machinists or engineers at home. Finally, the money that pays for more bombers that the nation doesn't need must come out of the budget for something else—schools, highways, health, whatever.

Nothing important is likely to change until politicians finally grasp what those B-2 workers already understand. Pumping up the weapons budget may boost share price for the surviving arms companies, but it no longer delivers much in the way of jobs for constituents back home. The military-industrial complex is awesomely resourceful, its power deeply rooted in the life of the nation, but it will not survive if the political system finally understands this new reality. The facts argue for a fundamental shift in national priorities, for a real demobilization now that the Cold War is ended. The hard politics of making those deep changes remains very difficult to face.

At Palmdale, I ask the company people what happens if Congress doesn't order any more B-2s. The plant spokesman, Allan Muller, cheerily replies: "We turn off the lights and hand the keys back to the Air Force and say, 'It's been nice working with you.'"

PART
III

◄○►

CHAPTER EIGHT

THE FUTURE OF WAR

O N THE DIMPLED PRAIRIE THAT IS FORT HOOD, Texas, the Fourth Mechanized Infantry Division has scattered fighting elements across the empty range to explore the future of war. The Blue team, the "good guys" in U.S. Army mock battles, is fielding a force of twelve thousand vehicles, from M-1 tanks to Avenger mobile rocket launchers, plus specially equipped foot soldiers flown in from Fort Lewis, Washington, for the exercises. All of them are "wired"—linked from top to bottom by a new, cyber-hip, satellite communications system. And at this moment, they are kicking the crap out of the Republic of Crasnovia.

Crasnovia is the old Army, still doing battles the old way, and the mood inside its field headquarters is decidedly fatalistic. Its TOC (Tactical Operations Center) is a large assembly of olive-drab field tents set up in a hilltop grove and draped with camouflage netting. The staff officers inside are still using the standard field radios or land-laid telephone lines to communicate with their units dispersed across the prairie. When action is reported from the field, the new battle positions are marked on acetate overlays covering the terrain maps. This battle, one might say, pits grease pencils against the Internet.

My escort officer, Major Dave Huebner, points to the Crasnovia battle plan, labeled "Object Death," and explains today's play: the Red forces are preparing to launch another southward attack against the Blues later in the day, so now they're sending out reconnaissance units that will locate the Blue tanks and direct artillery fire at them. "Reconnaissance and counter-reconnaissance—that's where the battle is won, time and time again," says Major Huebner, who commanded a tank in the Gulf War. A Crasnovian operations officer interjects with a slight correction.

"Sir, all of our mounted division reconnaissance was killed last night," Captain Chris Worril explains. The Blues nailed them with their UAV (Unmanned Aerial Vehicle), a small surveillance drone that stays aloft for hours, circling over the battlefield and bouncing data back to the Blues' TOC. Even in the darkness, the heat-sensing and infrared technology can pick out every moving motor vehicle on the field, identify friend and foe, then target the bad guys with ground-based, precision-guided missiles. Once the recon vehicles were wiped out, Crasnovia sent out "dirt teams" of scouts on foot. Three of them have survived, Captain Worril says, and are hiding somewhere on the prairie.

"As far as fighting on the ground, I don't think their maneuver units are any better than ours," Worril explains. "But because of their information advantage, they're able to put a lot more firepower on us."

On another scrubby hillside, a mile or so away, the Blue TOC seems a much more cheerful place. After all, they're winning. "Two days of attack, and we attrited the enemy division down to about 25 percent," Captain Barry Venable reports.

Plus, the good guys have all the best toys. Their operations tent is lit up by a galaxy of video screens, electronic display maps, and computer terminals, a command center that glows like the producer's booth in a television studio. Artillery fire, air defense, field intelligence, troop movements, even weather reports are visible on the electronic boards. (And CNN plays on a TV set in the corner, picked off a commercial satellite.) A main battle map unifies all this data in real time. Tanks and other elements are displayed as small blue and red icons, advancing or disappearing as they maneuver or "kill" each other.

A tank commander driving across the battlefield can punch up this same animated map inside his M-1 tank, as can an infantry squad leader carrying a small hand-held computer screen. Commanders at scattered locations use the map to consult on tactics electronically. "Like Johnny Madden drawing his plays on the TV screen," an officer explains.

All this is part of what the Army calls Force XXI—the first rough draft for a "digitalized Army" that, in theory, will be smarter and faster, smaller but more lethal, because it knows so much. The Fourth Infantry Division's assignment is to experiment with new hardware and tactics. The tactical Internet system they're testing today mimics the information revolution that is transforming civilian life.

"What we're trying to do," Huebner says, "is take the digital communications of a thirty-story office building and put the equivalent of E-mail in a thousand vehicles in the field. Only

123

what you've got in your office is hardwired to the wall and in a controlled environment. We're putting this system in mobile vehicles in an environment that, if it isn't wet and muddy, it's dusty."

"Gain information dominance." "Shape the battle space." "Use the global information environment." A new military lexicon has already developed to describe this new vision of warfare—wars that will presumably be fought with much smaller forces because information will empower soldiers to control much larger chunks of territory and sustain them with leaner, just-in-time supply lines. "Commanders can take more risks," the major says. "They don't necessarily need three brigades to hold the line because one brigade can do the job."

"It's just like Nintendo," says First Sergeant Jon Clark, a non-commissioned officer in charge of a unit of "Duck Hunters" deployed down the hill. These are Bradley fighting vehicles equipped with Avenger air defense missiles. The gunner inside simply looks at an electronic screen that displays—and identifies—the air traffic across forty square kilometers. "He can scroll over to the target he wants, and the system then swings the turret around to put the missile on that target," Clark says. "All he has to do is punch a button."

One alluring promise of electronic warfare—often invoked in the promotional literature and earnestly repeated by field officers—is that fewer Americans will die. If the gunners know exactly whom they're shooting at, fewer good guys will be killed by "friendly fire"—the fratricide that was the leading cause of U.S. casualties in Desert Storm. That is the theory anyway.

But meanwhile, down at the grunt level, the future isn't working. Not yet anyway. On a wooded slope a few miles from Blue headquarters, the infantrymen of C Company, First Battalion, Fifth Regiment, are spread out in small clusters among the scrawny live oak trees. As I approach, they are explaining to Force XXI field investigators why this high-tech stuff is too high-tech. "Definitely not user-friendly at our level," a staff sergeant says.

Charlie Company's twenty-three-year-old communications chief, Specialist Fourth-class Justin Campbell, is wrestling in the dust with the huge backpack—computer, digital radios, and assorted other electronics—that he must tote. "This is our third field exercise, and it's not getting any lighter," Campbell says. "Whatever they claim, I say it weighs closer to sixty-five pounds, because I have to carry it. That's not including the batteries, and you have to keep changing them."

While he discusses the merits and deficits of the new system, singsong voices arise from somewhere in the trees up the hillside. "Campbell! Campbell! We're in the *dark*, Campbell!" When the system goes down, the troopers call for Campbell to come fix it.

"I'm pretty popular," he says with a shrug. "A lot of the users are older NCOs who are not from the Nintendo generation. They're having a lot of trouble. Myself, I have confidence in the radio. The rest"—he laughs—"needs work."

It's all experimental, the officer emphasizes. Indeed, the "Land Warrior" vision that defense companies are working up for infantrymen bears a crude hint of an Arnold Schwarzenegger fantasy. A laser-guided rifle will see in the dark and target the body heat of enemy soldiers. Four sensors on a soldier's helmet will sound an alarm when he himself is being targeted by an enemy's laser. A tiny monocular eyepiece attached to the helmet swings down and allows a squad leader to read his electronic mail while he's slogging forward.

His helmet also carries a miniaturized TV camera that sends live video back to headquarters. The idea is that a general behind the lines can see exactly what the grunts are seeing as they charge into battle. This might give new meaning to that famous battle cry of the American Revolution: "Don't shoot till you see the whites of their eyes."

Only what the general may see instead are the whites (and browns) of GI bare butts. During boring interludes in the Fort Hood exercises, some C Company troopers amuse themselves by shooting dirty videos—and sending them up the chain of command. "They've been taking some pretty raunchy pictures," Campbell says. Like what? "Use your imagination." Then he adds: "Fortunately, the system isn't working very well, so I don't think those pictures are really making it to higher up."

The whole concept needs work—evidently a lot more work. The exercises at Fort Hood are only a warm-up for much more rigorous mock battles that are staged several months later at the

Army's National Training Center at Fort Irwin, California. During those encounters in the Mojave Desert, the First Brigade from the Fourth Division gets shellacked—one win, one tie, and six losses, according to one accounting. There's no shame in the losing performance since the experienced regular forces at Fort Irwin are fully familiar with the terrain and nearly always defeat the visiting units. That's not what disturbs the Force XXI planners.

The post-action report on the Fort Irwin battles finds that, instead of faster and smarter, the digitalized Army is slower, more fragile, *and* more vulnerable. Tactical Internet, with its related data feeds, the report states, "is not yet a coherent, stable system." The foot soldiers' digital equipment is (as Specialist Campbell observed) "still rejected by the light infantry because of weight, battery life, light discipline." The frequent breakdowns of the system require dozens of contractor representatives to stay in the battle zone so they can repair their companies' equipment. "There was no discernible increase in tempo of Blue operations. . . . Several operations centers reported it was slower than normal, especially in movements."

The worst news, however, is about casualties: the Blues suffer more than normal, not fewer, particularly from their own weapons. "There was no discernible increase in Blue survivability," the observers report. ". . . There was a large *increase* in the number of fratricide events."

One explanation is that Blue Force troops evidently walked into their own widely spread minefields. Another is that the

Blue units firing the anti-armor missiles took out some of their own vehicles at long range. Overall, the Blue Force suffered three times the average level of fratricide from previous training exercises fought by conventional means.

Force XXI goes back to the drawing boards. The future is not yet.

◄o►

Confronted with peace and deprived of a convincing enemy, the military imagination leaps ahead to fight the next war. Across many centuries, this has always been the case between the big wars. Peace is an anxious lull when warrior dreams are agitated by techno-visionaries and the industrial ambitions of weapons makers. Sometimes they get it right, and the result is a fundamental breakthrough in war-fighting, like radar or rocket engines.

Sometimes the triumphant generals become so enthralled by their own sense of superiority that the magnificent delusions they construct eventually destroy them. After World War I, the victorious French Army built the fortifications known as the Maginot Line and declared that this innovation would repel German invasions for all time. Hitler sent his tanks around it and marched straight into Paris. Peacetime, in other words, can be dangerous for a nation if it fosters illusions of invincibility.

In any case, designing the war of the future sets up another point of collision with the past. Even if futuristic ideas prove to be sound, the Pentagon and the arms industry are still reluctant to give up what already exists—the vast arsenal of conventional overkill. They cannot have it both ways, one would think, but so far they are doing their best to accomplish just that, with very little resistance from the political system. So the process of elaborating a future world of utterly new war-fighting weapons proceeds, even as companies prepare to turn out new generations of the conventional, and even as the armed services struggle to maintain readiness with the existing arsenal.

Right now, the American military establishment claims to be in the midst of a "revolution in military affairs" (or RMA, in the Pentagon's shorthand). This technological upheaval, it is said, will transform every aspect of warfare and eclipse most of the conventional armaments that now exist. The Army's effort to create "wired" ground forces is only one dimension of RMA, a modest first step toward much larger concepts. The inspiration, of course, is the industrial revolution in global commerce—the efficiency and precision made possible by the new electronic technologies. The high-tech vision was made more fashionable by the U.S. victory in the Gulf War, with its video clips of precision bombing and scant American casualties.

War will become "capital-intensive and automated," as one analyst puts it. Instead of nose-to-nose ground battle between contending armies, the action will become increasingly long-range, dispersed, and depersonalized—fought with deep-strike precision missiles, information dominance, even space-based weaponry (though now prohibited by treaty) using exotic

129

energy forces like particle beams to kill or immobilize. As the electronic systems take over war-fighting roles, the human ranks in uniform will be downsized—just like civilian workforces—and the fighters will need to become much smarter.

"The future Army will really need sort of super-soldiers who can operate in this really difficult environment—not just fighting other soldiers but also fighting the other side's system, which can now 'acquire' them at greater range," says Michael G. Vickers, director of strategic studies at the Center for Strategic and Budgetary Assessments, a Pentagon-financed think tank in Washington. "I served on a Defense Science Board study last year that looked at this issue: could five thousand men do what fifty thousand men did before? Not in all cases, but with the right things, you could substitute automation for these large forces. Then maybe a soldier will need to fight in much smaller groups. But he will control more territory than he could in the past."

In this scenario, for instance, micro-robots become scouts and even the warriors—miniaturized mechanical creatures that carry sensors forward into difficult, dangerous terrain and someday guns or explosives. "These things are on the horizon right now," Vickers says. "Some of them look kind of like Slinkies. They have an easy locomotion and can crawl pretty good and go over rough stuff and into small places. So in a high-end war, the super-soldiers might number only fifty thousand, but you still might have a four-hundred-thousand-man army because your support requirements go up as you get more technical. Even if the robots and all that stuff are your war-fighters, someone's got to maintain these things."

Saddam Hussein's ill-fated venture in Kuwait demonstrated that the traditional tank invasion is indeed obsolete—if the other side has air superiority and high-tech dominance in electronic intelligence and precision missiles. But the Gulf War also prompted chilling reflection among U.S. military thinkers: maybe these same technological elements will someday make *our* weapons obsolete, too. The so-called platforms that carry the firepower and are the backbone of modern warfare—tanks, surface ships, and aircraft—are all vulnerable in different ways to deep-strike weapons and electronic surveillance systems. If a cruise missile can take out Iraqi tanks, why not American aircraft carriers? Or air bases? Or cities?

Good grief. Maybe America isn't ready for the next war, after all—despite its burgeoning arsenal, despite the $250 billion it spends every year on defense, and despite the fact that no other industrial nation challenges U.S. status as the world's only superpower. The thought excites a search for exotic new forms of armaments.

The Navy dreamed up the arsenal ship—a huge barge that carries five hundred missiles and looks like the *Monitor* and the *Merrimac,* the original ironclad ships that first dueled during the American Civil War. Its supposed advantage is that vast firepower can be floated around the world with a crew of only fifty, compared to fifty-five hundred on an aircraft carrier.

The downside eventually dawned on naval planners: this barge would be just as vulnerable as the carriers already are. Maybe it could somehow be made "stealthy" and elude radar, like the B-2 bomber. Vickers says Europeans are experimenting with the idea of generating ocean mists to protect ships from easy detection. If that doesn't work, then the arsenal barge might have to be submersible—that is, a huge submarine loaded with hundreds of missiles. This sounds a lot like the preexisting Trident submarine.

The Air Force imagines opportunity in the high-tech threat. With the use of space sensors, stealth, and other innovations, it is trying once again to claim a preeminent role for air power and suggesting, none too subtly, that ground and naval forces will soon be obsolete. (Military pilots have been making this argument, unsuccessfully, for approximately seventy years.) On the other hand, Air Force officers are aghast at the suggestion that future wars will not require even pilots.

Lockheed Martin circulates an artist's rendering of the fighter plane of the future—it looks just like the F-16 the company already manufactures at its Fort Worth plant. The only differences are that the sleek, gray plane in the illustration carries twelve air-to-air missiles under its wings (an F-16 can carry only four at most) and there's no pilot, only smooth fuselage where the cockpit is supposed to be. It's called the UCAV (Uninhabited Combat Aircraft Vehicle). Other major defense companies are working on their own conceptions of the same product.

"I'm a technologist, an engineer," says Lockheed's Dr. Armand J. Chaput as he explains the UCAV's potential. "My job is not to determine what the government wants but what the government will need and will want only it doesn't know it yet." The armed services are developing larger long-distance reconnaissance planes that fly without pilots, so the logical next step is to outfit similar unmanned aircraft with missiles or bombs. The UCAVs will have "pilots," but they sit safely on the ground, "flying" the aircraft from a computer terminal back at the air base.

"The concept of war is different now," Chaput explains. "The kind of war you become involved in now is where the national image is at stake and not necessarily the national security. So you want to be present and engaged, but for God's sake, don't let any American boys and girls get killed. The other constraint is the budget: how do you do more with less? The concept of UCAVs didn't have anything to do with fighter planes at first. It was about developing reusable weapons."

"There's a market niche for the UCAV between the Tomahawk cruise missile and fighter planes," he explains. The cruise missiles are a very expensive way to deliver explosives to a target—about $1,500 per pound for the Tomahawk. But the government "is still going to want to use them, because no pilots will be lost of captured," Chaput says. "It's kind of the CNN factor." A UCAV will perform the same role as a cruise missile, but after it dumps its explosives, it can fly home to be used again.

By Lockheed's calculations, the cost of operations and ground support could be drastically reduced if the Air Force shifted battlefield bombing to these riderless drones. While operating a squadron of fighter planes consumes $50 million, an equivalent force of UCAVs modeled on the F-16 would cost only $10 million. A smaller version of the UCAV with a flying-wing design would operate even more cheaply. Not everyone, however, buys the optimistic economic analysis.

"The problem is, they're just wildly expensive, incredibly expensive," insists William D. O'Neil, vice president of the Center for Naval Analyses and himself a former director of strategic planning at Lockheed. "For one thing, the average UAV only lasts about ten flights. We've been flying them for years, and we've got data. When you're flying an airplane, you have lots of little things go wrong, and without thinking about it, you adjust and compensate for the problems. But the UAV doesn't do that. The UAV will just continue according to its program as it spirals out of control. So they crash at a great rate. They like to talk about UAVs that will only cost $1 million, but if it only lasts ten flights, that's $100,000 per flight."

Even if the UCAV overcomes the problem of frequent crashes, a large cultural barrier stands in its way: Air Force esprit is rooted in the adventurous life of the pilot, not the computer operator. The notion that the ranks of active fliers will be thinned out by automation creates real anxiety. "Say I have an Air Force in the future with a fifty-fifty mix of manned and unmanned aircraft," Vickers muses. "Who should I promote as generals? At some point, the folks who figure out how to do UCAVs will become pretty important. That's when the cultural challenge will really come."

The much larger barrier to RMA, in all its various forms, is money. Whether or not these concepts represent the future of warfare, they are blocked by the status quo that consumes the Pentagon's money right now. Military leaders may like the idea of exploring futuristic concepts, but not if it means abandoning their present hardware or canceling the new stuff already lined up for production. The central dilemma facing the American military-industrial complex is that it can't pay for all of its present forces, much less for the futuristic dreams.

Last spring, while Defense Secretary William Cohen was drafting his quadrennial defense review to determine military priorities, Vickers's think tank ran an experiment in alternative thinking. (Called Transformational Strategy Game II, this exercise was also sponsored by the Pentagon.) A group of young colonels and other midlevel officers were asked to resolve the same budget dilemma facing Cohen and the Joint Chiefs of Staff. The secretary of Defense cut back here and there on the margins but did not change the basic force structure of the armed services or cancel any of the major new weapons systems in the pipeline.

The colonels, however, proposed dramatic cutbacks in present forces and procurement in order to free up enough money to pay for serious research and development for future weapons systems. The Army, they concluded, could cut three of its ten divisions and cancel plans for a self-propelled howitzer so that serious funding could be channeled into Force XXI and Land Warrior development. The Air Force could drop six fighter wings, retire the B-1 bomber, and cancel the Joint Strike Fighter so that it could finance two hundred UAV systems and buy twenty airborne lasers. If the Navy canceled construction of a new carrier and demobilized three carrier battle groups, it would have the money to build five arsenal ships and other futuristic systems.

Right or wrong, their conclusions sound like bold, new thinking, but no one expects any of their proposals to be put into action. "Between Congress, the industry, and the military, it's not going to be easy to pursue some of this innovation because there's no real champion for it," Vickers gloomily concedes. "We've got three big programs for new tactical aircraft planned for $350 billion plus, and industry wants to produce what it has—these multi-multi-billion-dollar manned aircraft projects—even though all these guys are lining up to say, 'Oh, we could design this new stuff if the Pentagon wants it.'

"It will be very hard to make this happen. It will take a military leader or a Congress that wants to save money. Then industry will say, 'Sure, if this is what you want, we'll produce it for you.' But the companies are not going to leap up and stick their necks out right away." Some military leaders, he adds, are reluctant to admit publicly that the force structure can be reduced substantially because they fear the freed-up funds would not go to weapons innovations but to other public priorities.

There's also a well-earned skepticism among senior field commanders who remember crackpot high-tech ideas that failed in previous eras. During the Vietnam War, Defense Secretary Robert McNamara naively proclaimed that an "electronic battlefield" of sensors was going to defeat the enemy. The Vietcong went right around it, as did the North Vietnamese Army. The generals and admirals also know that the precision bombing against Iraq was not nearly as precise as advertised. The General Accounting Office estimates that the accuracy rate in the Gulf War was more like 45 percent, not the 85 percent the Pentagon originally claimed.

"The people who have the day-to-day responsibility for trying to make sure that operational commitments are met are pretty skeptical about a lot of these purist, blue-sky notions," says William O'Neil.

The logic of new technology is so alluring and promising, he warns, that it leaves out the hard economics. "We live in a world where the gap between what's feasible from a technological standpoint and what's affordable seems to be growing," he observes. "Everybody, not just us, is spending less on defense, not more. And the price of the things you have to buy for defense continues to go up. The Soviet Union bankrupted itself with a defense establishment that was crazy in proportion to the resources they had. I don't see very many other countries that are eager to do that."

In fact, a deadly irony is embedded in the potential of these new technologies: smaller, poorer nations may be able to defend themselves, on the cheap, against the intrusion of America's overwhelming military strength. They can do so if they are willing to adopt various nasty defense systems and spend their money smartly. A country can build a defensive barrier by using chemical or biological weapons (not to mention loose nukes available from the former Soviet Union). It can purchase lots of cruise missiles from the global arms bazaar's open market for as little as $10,000 apiece.

A still-classified study by the Defense Science Board concludes that a regional adversary, by spending $10 billion a year on defense and such things as missiles, commercial space satellites, and hardened underground facilities, could insulate itself against a U.S. invasion. "They could really screw up our current forces," Vickers concedes. "They could develop a capability that would hurt our military as it is currently planned, but it would also hurt all this new stuff. It's not a panacea, it's just a different kind of war."

The abstract logic of fighting future wars with revolutionary new technologies has a pristine, bloodless quality that is attractive. The trouble is that real war is never so neat and always bloody.

138

CHAPTER NINE

◄◦►

OTHER VOICES

I F AMERICA WERE IN THE MOOD TO RETHINK ITS AWE-
SOME MILITARY ESTABLISHMENT, PEOPLE WOULD BE
LISTENING TO SENATOR JOHN MCCAIN, A POLITICAL
reformer with the warrior's heroic credentials. McCain is a Naval
Academy graduate and former Navy pilot who flew bombing mis-
sions during the war in Indochina. He was shot down over North
Vietnam and spent six years as a prisoner-of-war in the "Hanoi
Hilton," undergoing torture and other abuses.

Now the Cold War is over, and McCain is Arizona's senior
senator, a conservative Republican with provocative ideas about
how to reshape the defense forces. Hardly anybody wants to
hear them.

"I go on the talk shows all the time," McCain says. "You start
talking about national defense or foreign policy, the lines don't
light up. Talk about Medicaid, Social Security, IRS, taxes—
bang!—they all want to be heard."

Within the armed services, there is at least a modest low-
volume debate under way about the nature of future wars and
what's needed for national security. Within the political establishment, there is grand evasion and parochial game-playing.

"I think we're stuck for several reasons," the senator says, "and
one of the major reasons is that most Americans don't care. The
Cold War is over. There's no perceived threat, the economy is

good. Fewer and fewer Americans join the military. Politicians naturally gravitate to what interests their constituents. Because the people don't care, there's all sorts of political mischief being performed. And we're not making the transition to the post–Cold War era."

The senator's website shows a pig rolling a barrel of dollars across the screen—the political pork that gets tucked into annual defense appropriations bills and that he tries to knock out. (President Clinton also eliminated some with his line-item veto, which has now, however, been declared unconstitutional.) Congress each year commits billions more than the Pentagon has requested, especially in election years. It refuses to close any more military bases and protects civilian employees at inefficient arsenals and depots. It finds the cash for expensive relics from the Cold War while it shrinks federal programs for people.

"If this were the Cold War, you'd find no greater advocate for the Sea Wolf submarine and the B-2 bomber than John McCain," the senator says. "There was a real threat, a real need. But now . . . are you going to launch a $2 billion airplane on a tactical strike against Iraq? I mean, God, what's the point here?"

Senator McCain is among the stout-hearted voices who are trying to articulate alternative visions of defense, despite the general indifference. What follows is a glimpse of the great debate that America ought to be having with itself, reflected in three very different voices. This is the new thinking you might be hearing if political leaders or the major media were listening.

There's nothing very radical in John McCain's thinking. Like some others, he is trying to work his way through the new realities and reconcile the obvious contradictions. The central contradiction (described in part I) is well understood among budget experts: even though it's spending $250 billion a year on defense, the United States cannot possibly pay for all of its military commitments.

"The money just isn't there," McCain concludes. "And the problems are exacerbated when you spend $2 billion on a B-2 or $3.5 billion to $4 billion on a submarine. Then you can't maintain readiness. You can't buy the equipment to modernize. You can't maintain the ability for rapid deployment around the globe."

McCain's solutions include big hits on the status quo. He would start by jettisoning the Pentagon's present strategy of being prepared to fight two major regional wars at once. One war at a time is plenty, he thinks, and more believable to any adversaries. Once the official fictions are abandoned, the force structure itself can be made rational—smaller and more affordable. For starters, McCain would reassess the array of overseas deployments, case by case, and cancel many of them, relying instead on the military's ability to project forces rapidly anywhere in the world.

McCain would also whack some cherished weapons systems. Right now, for instance, the Pentagon intends to launch three new major combat aircraft—the F-22 for the Air Force, the F-

18/E and F-18/F for the Navy, and then the Joint Strike Fighter designed for both. An old Navy pilot, McCain thinks the F-18 is sound. He's skeptical of the other two.

"One thing, I think, is obvious," the senator says. "You cannot have all three weapons systems move forward. You're going to have to cancel one of them—at least. I don't know which one that is, but just look at the budget: you're going to consume two-thirds of the defense procurement budget just on tactical aircraft."

The Navy, he adds, ought to give up its ambitious plans to build a new class of attack submarines, replacing "the current, very capable attack submarine force with an all-new class of stealthy, high-technology submarines." The new subs might have made sense against the Soviets, but the need has "diminished significantly."

The Army's large ground forces, meanwhile, must shrink in size, he thinks. As offshore deployments are reduced, allied nations should assume the burden of providing the troops for peacekeeping in local conflicts, especially in Europe. McCain likes the promise of the new technologies but rejects grandiose claims that ships, tanks, and planes are now obsolete.

"Historically speaking, whenever we have won a significant victory, there's always been this idea that we can do away with those expensive pieces of hardware and go to some scenario where we can win wars on the cheap," he says. "I just don't think so."

The keystone of McCain's reform thinking is acknowledging a new fact of life: a real war, large or small, is now a lot less likely

for the United States. That assumption justifies his central proposal: a system of "tiered readiness" for the uniformed services.
Instead of keeping the entire force of one and a half million constantly primed for war-fighting, America could safely reduce the
readiness level for many military units into three tiers of training
and preparedness. If things do heat up in the world, second- and
third-tier troops could be rapidly brought up to full fighting
condition.

Does anyone salute this idea? It's "strenuously resisted," the
senator concedes with a shrug. The Navy is open to "tiered
readiness" because it resembles what the Navy already does with
its ship rotations. The Army, McCain observes, "is emotionally
and viscerally opposed because it would cut their budget."

That's the objective, of course. "These situations are a series
of bad choices," McCain explains. "I'd like to maintain every
military unit at 100 percent readiness, even if it's the National
Guard in Window Rock, Arizona. But when you look at the
budget realities, there's an enormous amount of money to be
saved by allowing some units to reduce their state of readiness if
they are not going to be called up to fight right away. Otherwise,
I don't know where the money comes from."

The senator, a veteran of the tragedy in Vietnam, has a central
conviction that would allow the United States to reduce its military forces: America cannot play imperial policeman for the
world. McCain opposed U.S. engagement in Bosnia initially,
also in Somalia and Haiti, arguing that American troops could

not be expected to remedy those troubled conditions. Nor did he see the national interest at stake.

"American troops should not be ordered into a conflict unless U.S. vital interests are threatened," McCain declared in a speech to conservative activists earlier this year. "This is the primary distinction between the role of a great power and that of a policeman. . . . While we all hope for a world in which justice and law govern the actions of states, it would be self-destructive hubris for the United States to put the lives of its soldiers at risk for the sole purpose of good citizenship in the international community."

◄○►

Gary Hart, the former Colorado senator and Democratic presidential contender, worries about a different kind of vulnerability: the threat to American democracy posed by its own large and permanent military establishment. It's not that Hart fears a Latin America–style generals' coup. The danger he sees is the widening divide between Washington governing elites, both political and military, and Americans at large. When Washington sends troops off to war zones without a full, frank debate on the objectives and potential costs, citizens are left ignorant and impotent. Someday, when an intervention goes awry, this elite decision-making will generate a political crisis.

"The isolation of the military from society is unhealthy at best and dangerous at worst," Hart writes in his book *The Minuteman*. He proposes a radical solution: revive the tradition of citizen soldiers that existed before the Cold War fostered permanent mobilization. Shrink the regular forces drastically to one-quarter or one-third of their present size. Then let regulars train and supervise a well-equipped, well-trained volunteer force in the reserves and National Guard.

This shift would save many billions, but the larger purpose is to reengage the broad American public in questions of national defense—the why and wherefore of going to war. If something like this doesn't happen, Hart foresees an explosive collision ahead. At a Washington forum, he warned the audience of policy thinkers: "The assumption in this town is that, once the political and military leaders make a decision to use the military, the American people will follow with their lives and their checkbooks. This is an elitist assumption, and I think it is ending."

Hart's critique echoes the political turmoil of the Cold War years, especially during the ill-fated intervention in Vietnam when millions of citizens rebelled. Gary Hart was active then in antiwar politics and managed Senator George McGovern's 1972 presidential campaign. Elected to the Senate two years later, he surprised both friends and adversaries by seeking a seat on the Armed Services Committee, where he became a respected voice on reforming military affairs. Now a lawyer for international business, he, too, is trying to provoke a larger debate.

During the Persian Gulf War, Hart says, American soldiers were essentially used like modern Hessians—a "mercenary army" hired to defend the decadent royal families of Kuwait and

Saudi Arabia. The rhetoric was about freedom, but the real issue was access to cheap oil. The political establishment finds it easier to deploy military force in behalf of entrenched economic interests, he observes, than to confront the deeper changes required in energy consumption and production. Sooner or later, he expects the evasion to blow up in America's face.

"What happens if we wake up some morning and the Saudi royal family is overthrown?" Hart asks. "Our energy policy collapses. We will be in the desert again. And it won't be for six months."

The situation reminds him of the famous warning from President Dwight Eisenhower, back in 1958, about the military-industrial complex's encroaching political influence. "This is Eisenhower's nightmare," Hart asserts. "The military-industrial complex is dug in to defend economic interests that have nothing to do with national defense."

The Gulf War provided some supporting evidence for Hart's "citizen soldier." The Desert Storm force included some 230,000 reserve forces, and their performance, especially in supporting roles like airlift, was impressive and widely praised. On the other hand, the call-up of reserves did not provoke the lively debate on foreign policy objectives that Hart envisions, perhaps because the enemy was so inept and only 157 Americans died.

"Sooner or later," Hart predicts, "people are going to ask: Why do we have to have this huge military structure? Why do we have to spend $250 billion a year for a Bosnia, Haiti, or

146

Somalia? I don't know anybody in this town who has an answer for that question. It's only a matter of time before someone gets up and says: 'The emperor has no clothes.'"

—◦—

Compared to Washington's usual policy wonks, Michael Vlahos is clearly over the top. When I first met the forty-six-year-old political scientist, he was dressed downtown—black jacket and slacks, black T-shirt and loafers—the right look for downtown Manhattan, but not D.C. During the Reagan years, Vlahos flourished as a Cold War policy thinker and got his ticket punched at all the right places, from the CIA to the State Department. In the 1990s, he collaborated closely with Representative Newt Gingrich on new ideas before he grasped that Gingrich's revolutionary talk was bogus.

Now he is utterly disillusioned with the governing elites and thus liberated from conventional thinking. These days, Michael Vlahos turns out intriguing, troubling, visionary essays on the future of war and why this new age is profoundly threatening for America, though not for the usual reasons.

"I have to say something that will sound terrible but may still be true," he begins. "We, the United States, may become the Darth Vader wearing the black helmet. We've created an industrial system that works for us and some allies but is imperial and seems oppressive to many others. We increasingly will find ourselves in the same position as empires of the past, the Persians and Romans, Spain under Phillip II, the British in the late nine-

147

teenth century. Any great empire trying to ride herd on the world in an age of major change is in danger."

The prognosis sounds apocalyptic and a bit elusive in the details, but Vlahos is trying to provoke a sober reading of history. Empires fall or are eclipsed, not because they are weak in the traditional terms, but because they fail to grasp the future—the new social and political realities spawned by their very own economic power and invention. In a high-octane essay in the spring 1998 issue of the *Washington Quarterly,* entitled "The War After Byte City," Vlahos compares the hubris of American leaders to the arrogant French and British generals who got their comeuppance in the distant past:

> We are in the midst of an economic upheaval equivalent to the industrial revolution in its capacity to transform our lives. . . . But America's ruling elites have defined a world system that does not allow for the possibility of Big Change. Like the French plutocrats of the 1850s, the old Cold War establishment is pledged to preserve the old paradigm—meaning, centrally, itself. . . . Shorn of its entitling Cold War, the U.S. ruling establishment now wishes to extend the *noblesse oblige* necessary to manage an unruly world—at all costs. It defines the United States as the *status quo power,* its sacred word is *stability* and its imperative verb is to *manage.*

The Big Change that preoccupies Vlahos is the developing "Infosphere" that was largely invented by America—future communications in cyberspace that will create new social and

148

business relationships and unknowable shifts in political power. This new information age will certainly generate new dimensions of warfare, but Vlahos thinks the truly revolutionary impact will be the social transformations—people buying and selling, meeting and forming affinities in cyberspace, beyond the reach of established power. That is the subversive nature of the future, the upheaval that threatens U.S. domination.

"War is going to happen when new groups are struggling to be liberated and established forces are holding them down," he explains. "Part of what makes war so compelling is the ritual of a newly arising identity—people who contrast themselves with the alien other and, in the act of triumphing over the forces in black, define themselves as the force in white."

What groups? What people? Vlahos cannot say, of course, but he suggests they may not even be nations. The Infosphere, once its technologies reach full potential, can unite religious and ethnic interests or like-minded economic players across the usual boundaries. Their power would not necessarily be grounded in traditional armies and weaponry but perhaps in their ability to manipulate information itself.

Information war gives an example of what Vlahos means:

Everything's going to be mixed up, once the Infosphere is part of everyone's daily life. It's not going to be possible for the military to seal them off and keep them out. Even today people can invade the system and disrupt it and listen to it. Let's say you've got forces out there, fighting some pipsqueak, but you've lost control of the information system. You don't know whether they're listening and how much they've penetrated your command and control. So you don't know whether what you're seeing on the screen is correct or even real. You don't know where the enemy really is. If you fire a missile, you don't know where it's really going to go, who you're going to hit.

The Pentagon is well aware of this technological nightmare and presumably at work on the problem. But what Vlahos is describing may not be fixable by a superpower if the global information system truly operates with open access for all, unless the military intends to shut it down (or maybe build a parallel universe of its own). In any case, Vlahos is skeptical of the military imagination.

"The great debates in the Pentagon are over the next weapons systems—the next carrier, the next fighter aircraft—all in the context that we are already the most powerful nation," he observes. "People believe in RMA because they haven't understood the totality of change. What they understand is the cliché of change."

The essential vulnerability that Vlahos identifies is not technological but political. It is the intangible conflict between superpower America's desire to manage the world versus this era's historic imperative for profound change. Having invented many of the new technologies, the United States has an obvious head start in exploiting them. Yet its leaders also want to control things in order to preserve the status quo. What America needs is not more armaments, Vlahos concludes, but a new national dynamic that fosters a culture of adaptability.

"We're not going to build a splendid new Battle Star system," he says. "But we can change the atmosphere of thought. Instead of saying we're going to kick butt, we should say: 'We're going to get ready for what comes down the road and prevent tradition from leading us into defeat.'"

This task is always difficult, especially for triumphant empires. The heavy weight of the status quo makes Vlahos feel gloomy. "It does seem, right now, that nobody can challenge us," he muses. "But I go back to the British in the late nineteenth century, when they had 50 percent of the world's GNP and they could trump anybody.

"But, you know, it didn't last very long, did it?"

CHAPTER TEN

"NO JUSTICE, NO PEACE"

PARANOIA WAS ALWAYS A VITAL ELEMENT IN COLD WAR IDEOLOGY, AND FEARFUL ALARMS WERE REGU-LARLY ANNOUNCED ABOUT OTHERS IN THE WORLD threatening America. If South Vietnam were lost to the Communists, it was said, their next stop would be San Francisco. If Nicaragua became a Soviet outpost in our hemisphere, Reagan told us, the enemy would soon be marching on Texas. It seems bizarre now, even silly, that citizens of the richest nation on earth could be so easily spooked.

Nor has the paranoia entirely vanished. Former Secretary of Defense Caspar Weinberger, who presided over the Reagan arms buildup, published a book in 1997, *The Next War*, that recites a hallucinatory list of scary scenarios. China and North Korea invade South Korea *and* Taiwan in 1998, using nukes and biological weapons. Iran nukes Europe a year later. By 2003 the United States is compelled to invade Mexico to stamp out drugs and illegal immigrants. Then Russia launches a new campaign to conquer Europe, and Japan seizes control of oil and East Asia. These prospects, we are told, require another military buildup.

If Americans can get beyond the old insecurities, the end of the Cold War is a great opportunity to reimagine the world in new terms: a world without empires. A renewed system of international relations is possible now, one that is not controlled by the United States or anyone else. America could make itself the natural leader for achieving this historic transition. Or it could remain the status quo power, standing in the way of the future, suppressing change and accumulating resentment around the world.

The globalization of commerce and finance—marketing and production and investing—has created a great new opening for everyone as well as colossal potential for economic breakdown and nationalist conflict, even shooting wars. Like it or not, we are now connected to distant others—as buyers and sellers, as workers and investors. Are we building a new world of promise and equity or exploitation and anger? Right now, our awesome power is deployed to defend the rights of capital and commerce, but not human rights and people exploited by the global system.

The voluminous policy literature on fighting the next war scarcely acknowledges the war-and-peace implications of the globalizing economy. Nor does our government. Washington is putting up bailout aid of $3 billion for the deeply corrupt regime in Indonesia, which suppresses labor rights and other human freedoms. America's leading multinational corporations are building advanced-technology production for China on the backs of $60-a-month factory workers who are disciplined by Community Party cadres. The financial turmoil that recently devastated developing economies in Asia and Latin America looks like a Wall Street conspiracy to the victims in Malaysia or Thailand.

154

The point is made by Robert Borosage, director of the Campaign for America's Future, in the succinct phrase: "No justice, no peace." War arises from many sources, rational and irrational, but the weak will naturally find their enemy in the wealthy and powerful who are running the system, as Vlahos suggests. Borosage wrote recently in the *Boston Review:*

> In this extraordinary time, our focus should be on building the structures of peace—the harder, softer tasks of securing minimal decency, bolstering democracy and the rule of law, strengthening international peacekeeping and peacemaking institutions, and dealing with such real world causes of tension as economic upheaval, mass displacement, environmental catastrophe, resource rivalries, religious and nationalist passions.

In the turmoil of the post–Cold War peace, some things have not really changed. In national security, we have settled for a bit less of the same. What we really need is to rethink the whole idea.

Instead of concocting glamorous new weapons systems, Americans might move to higher ground and dream of a common humanity. Instead of searching the world for likely enemies, Americans should recognize that, in this new age, we are all riding in the same boat.

‑‹O›‑

CONCLUSION

I F AMERICANS WERE SOMEHOW PROVOKED INTO
ENGAGING IN A SERIOUS, SUSTAINED DEBATE ABOUT
NATIONAL DEFENSE, THEY MIGHT FIND THEMSELVES
returning to an old question. What was the Cold War about?
Naturally, it was about defending ourselves and allies against the
Soviets. But the mobilization drew its unifying energies from
deeper purposes as well.

Americans always saw their nation as the transcendent liberator, standing up for freedom in remote places, generously assist-
ing people in their efforts to get out from under totalitarian
regimes. But was the Cold War, as radical critics contended,
really about securing markets for U.S. commerce and finance?
In hindsight, we might accept that both motivations—national
values and American economic interests—were present in the
struggle. The United States was both virtuous and powerful,
righteous and self-interested.

To mention these old Cold War rationales opens up rich
questions about our present sense of purpose. Does America still
maintain its burgeoning military apparatus in order to advance
human freedoms? Or to protect the free flows of multinational
production and finance? Are we struggling to democratize the
globe or merely to clear a path for global corporations?

157

The contradictions become obvious. Purposes that coexisted compatibly throughout the Cold War now regularly come in conflict with one another. The global economic system, led by the United States, governs trade, financial markets, and the rights of capital by imposing complex rules but insists that fundamental human freedoms are not a legitimate basis for global regulation. Raising questions of environmental protection, labor rights, or social equity—not to mention the democratic principles of free speech and freedom of assembly—is described as an intrusion on the trading system, possibly even an impediment to the spread of prosperity. National sovereignty (including America's) is told to yield to the efficiencies of globalizing enterprises.

These contradictions are potentially explosive for America, I believe, because they feed a deep disconnect between the public's values and expectations and the assumptions held by the governing elites. Without a well-defined set of purposes, without the political discussions that might lead to a new national consensus, the country is drifting toward a collision that will expose its false obligations—open-ended commitments to possible military involvement that were never truly ratified by the American people or even fully recognized by them.

In the post–Cold War vacuum, the United States has gradually assumed the obligations of empire. Its military and economic powers are deployed as a kind of high-minded, vigilante enforcer of world order and global commerce. By a stroke of fate, we have become the sole, surviving superpower. So we remain prepared to go anywhere (if we choose) on behalf of maintaining the peace or challenging potential belligerents. Meanwhile, the United States continues as the leading global missionary for laissez-faire economics, pressuring rival economies to adopt the American way of doing business and banking.

The spirit of triumphalism is palpable, at least among financial and business elites. Imperial hubris is expressed when strategic thinkers justify military preparedness by identifying our new enemy, not as a given nation, but as "uncertainty." The Pentagon is told it must be ready to confront the limitless uncertainties of history.

Empire, even if benignly intended, assumes an infinite obligation to engage in defensive, police-like conflicts. The U.S. missile attacks on Afghanistan and Sudan assert a new privilege (one we would not likely grant to others). We are claiming the right to bomb any non-belligerent nation—instantly and without notice—if U.S. intelligence agencies decide threatening terrorists dwell there. This is a vast charter for employing America's high-tech military power, but it also suggests an above-the-law imperium. Do we imagine others will meekly accept our rule and never learn how to shoot back? I doubt the American public is on board for such an open-ended and bloody mission.

However, these public attitudes do not imply reactionary isolationism, as some pundits claim. In fact, you can make an argument that most citizens are more progressive—that is, truly internationalist—than their leaders. They want a "new world order" that would be genuinely new, not an American imperium.

If one steps back from establishment rhetoric, it is possible to see a profound contradiction in what the governing elites are pursuing. The national security imperative seeks to control unforeseen events anywhere in the world, while the global economic imperative tells governments to step back and cede their power to the marketplace. One purpose calls on the nation-state's military power; the other purpose claims that the nation-state is obsolete. Which is it to be—control or laissez-faire?

The two contrary directions come into conflict on many fronts, most notably in the new preoccupation with halting the spread of "NBC," or nuclear, biological, and chemical weapons. To do so, governments must impose rigorous technical regulations, inspections, and sanctions on both nations and businesses, while the same governments promote the deregulation of both domestic and international controls over commerce.

Business is business. When Iraqis develop forbidden weapons, we learn that it was made possible by the companies in Europe and America that sold start-up materials and equipment. When India detonates a nuclear bomb, the U.S. government responds by imposing harsh trade sanctions just as U.S. multinationals are launching a lobbying campaign to persuade Congress that such sanctions are ineffective, an intrusion on the trading system. India, for that matter, claims it was compelled to join the nuclear club because U.S. companies were selling so much advanced military technology to China, while China sold missile technology to Pakistan.

160

Such contradictions are ignored by treating national security and global economics as separate realms, a continuing conceit of presidents and policy makers. Meanwhile, the expanding reach of American dominion and obligation proceeds on both military and economic planes, regardless of such questions or the public's skepticism.

The International Institute for Strategic Studies, a London-based think tank, grandly describes the United States as the world's new "hyper-power." Like many other policy centers, the institute assumes that America will be there—must be there—for whatever unfolds. "For the management of serious crisis, it is always necessary for the U.S. to act," the institute declares. And, it is assumed, America will prevail if only it puts mind and muscle to whatever the situation. "Only the U.S. has the capacity to lead and, when it wishes to exercise the capacity to the full, it is able to dictate the terms on which solutions can be found," the IISS asserts.

American diplomats and military leaders would doubtless demur, especially about the Middle East. Yet they continue to act as if they believe their old press clippings, as if the United States still retains the power to dominate from the same position that it held throughout the Cold War. Events around the world suggest a slow but steady trend in the opposite direction, as large and small nations discover an ability to ignore the old emperor and do as they please.

What exactly have Americans signed up for? U.S. troops are already deployed as peacekeepers in the volatile territories of the former Yugoslavia, stuck there much longer than intended, hoping luck does not run out. Now these new national borders are being added to the commitment, while our new friend, Russia, gets isolated—via NATO expansion—and demonized once again. George Kennan, the original architect of Soviet containment fifty years ago, finds the ease with which American policy slipped on this new harness ominous.

"I think it is the beginning of a new Cold War," Kennan told the *New York Times*. "I think the Russians will gradually react quite adversely and it will affect their policies. I think it is a tragic mistake."

The Russians, he observed, were depicted during the Senate debate as still eager to invade Western Europe. "Don't people understand?" Kennan complained. "Our differences in the Cold War were with the Soviet Communist regime. And now we are turning our backs on the very people who mounted the greatest bloodless revolution in history to remove that Soviet regime."

The NATO expansion also evoked nostalgia for Cold War economics, since it keeps alive the wishful politics that sees defense production as a covert government jobs program. The desire to generate hometown jobs was denied by sponsors, of course, but the truth slipped out during the Senate debate.

In that debate, opponents offered an amendment that would put a cap on U.S. military subsidies for the process of absorbing the Czech Republic, Poland, and Hungary into the alliance. Everyone knows those nations are too poor to buy F-16s or high-tech military communications without lots of financial help from the other NATO nations. Senator Tom Harkin of Iowa proposed that the U.S. share be limited to no more than 25 percent of the total aid.

Senator Joseph I. Lieberman of Connecticut—where Pratt & Whitney builds jet engines for military aircraft—objected that Harkin's measure would "hurt American defense workers whose products will not be sold in these three countries."

"I thought this was about democracy," Harkin responded.

Lieberman retreated. "No, the overall debate is not about American workers," he agreed. "It's about the principles of freedom." Harkin's amendment lost, 76–24.

The other expansive dimension of America's global reach is its refreshed claim to economic hegemony. Since World War II and Bretton Woods, Washington has always seen itself as the prime protector and de facto governor of the global trading system, as well as the most dedicated champion of free-market reforms. Financial crisis and economic collapse in Asia, particularly Japan's deepening troubles, are feeding the elites' illusion that America is also in charge of the world's business.

With the U.S. Treasury setting strategy, the International Monetary Fund (IMF) is dispatched to make things right, restore financial order on behalf of global bankers, and teach those once-booming nations in Southeast Asia how to follow the American way. Leave aside that the IMF-Treasury prescriptions are doing more harm than good, as many critics contend.

What is already obvious, especially at a distance, is how crisis feeds prideful power.

The neo-imperial quality of the bailouts and reform packages is revealed in how intimately the overseers are willing to instruct other countries on the details of altering their business and banking structures. IMF supervisory teams are driving down the boulevard and pointing out which banks to close, telling proud nations which manufacturing conglomerates they must dismantle, how much to raise the price of food and fuel, where to cut government spending, employment, wages. Has a new raj claimed power over these developing peoples? If so, he is a bank examiner based in Washington, D.C.

In the long run, I suspect, national security will be much more influenced by these economic events than by how many active aircraft carriers are in the fleet or how many more B-2 bombers Congress decides to buy. The point is not to second-guess Washington's crisis decisions or commandments, but to suggest that a profound and potentially dangerous shift in relationships is under way in these events, at least in the balance of power perceived by Washington and Wall Street. After years of lauding and envying the "Asian miracle" in South Korea or Malaysia or Thailand, the American establishment abruptly dismisses it as a fraudulent failure.

One should be skeptical of these boasts. "Crony capitalism," after all, is not unknown to the United States; observe how politicians of both parties are financed by business patrons. Furthermore, transient claims about which nation has "won" the global economic contest have proved highly perishable in the past and usually disappear with changes in the business cycle.

Most important, American triumphalism obscures the unpleasant fact that, thanks to its large and persistent trade deficits, the United States has become the world's leading debtor nation. The accumulated national debt approaches $6 trillion, and the United States borrows huge sums from some of the very nations to whom it now teaches "sound economics." This is a most unnatural political condition, when a debtor presumes to scold its creditors.

If everything works out and general prosperity resumes, then the hydraulic forces of global capital markets may continue to prevail. If things go wrong and the global system deteriorates further, then unexpressed national resentments toward the new raj are sure to intensify and find expression. While they do not say so at present for obvious reasons, my hunch is that, from this crisis, battered Asian nations are developing a much less trusting perspective toward the United States. The most powerful economy seems to be an unreliable partner when things go wrong, willing to toss old friends over the side and impose harsh and self-interested discipline on them (then crow about American superiority).

If the United States proves to be an ineffective governor of the global system, then nations in recovery will seek out other arrangements—new alliances of economic power that give them more distance and independence from the center. Despite its financial debacle, Japan still retains brilliant manufacturing. In the Cold War years, it was content to be a passive partner to the United States while it accumulated market share and wealth. When the present crisis ends, it may decide to play a more independent hand.

Creditors do hold sway over their debtors—they can dump their bonds—and this ancient truth becomes clearer to all when the creditors decide to invoke it. Right now, it is not in anyone's interest to test the power relationships based on financial assets, but a time may come when Americans discover their own dependence, perhaps quite abruptly and harshly. This dimension of U.S. insecurity is not discussed among geopolitical thinkers, at least not in public, since economists have assured them that the nation's worsening debt position is not meaningful. They should reread the history of imperial Britain.

The end of the Cold War, furthermore, withdrew a veil from various aspects of the global economy that are unsettling because they offend American values. So long as the national struggle was focused on opposing Soviet hegemony around the world, a lot of contradictions could be ignored. Without the preoccupation with the Cold War, the economic system is exposed for inspection. Without the need for anti-Red military alliances, Americans can see that suppression of human freedom and other raw abuses of citizens also occur among some old allies.

Indonesia posed an immediate example. For years, Jakarta was the Potemkin village of global capitalism, the place statesmen and business leaders visited to celebrate the "Suharto miracle," just as Western socialists had been charmed by the Soviet Union's model communes earlier in the twentieth century. For thirty years, Indonesia's military regime served as a strategic ally in Southeast Asia as well as an emerging market for investment and low-wage production, not to mention oil.

Were American authorities hoodwinked about the true nature of Suharto's brutalities, like those beguiled socialists who came home from Russia proclaiming that communism works? I think the boosters were more cynical than deluded.

The Pentagon and the CIA maintained close relations with Suharto even though his government was always a fascist regime, that is, one that fuses military-business-political power. Multinational enterprises built many factories and banks there and paid the corrupt tolls (such as including the generals in joint ventures) for the privilege of access to Indonesia's cheap labor and burgeoning market.

In an oblique sense, the companies were reimbursed. While Suharto's cronies imposed irregular costs on doing business, the government also guaranteed that wages would be held artificially low, since any attempts to develop free trade unions or political opposition were smashed. This trade-off was not secret; everyone understood it. As recently as 1995, the United States averted its gaze while Suharto smashed a promising indepen-

167

dent labor movement, arrested its leaders, and charged them with subversion.

During the Cold War, this relationship worked for both sides (though not, of course, for exploited workers or for the promotion of democratic principles). Principle was sacrificed to strategic objectives, sowing the ground for future conflict. Now the system has begun to break up: economic crisis engulfed Suharto, and popular protests exposed the true nature of how he governed. If Indonesians are lucky, they may manage a gradual transition to a more open society. If unlucky, the unfolding power struggles could end in bloody civil war.

Which side are you on? In these new circumstances, the old labor question has become a national security issue. If Indonesia does descend into chaotic conflict, for instance, would U.S. military forces be expected to take a role in restoring order? If so, would they stand with the military commanders whom they helped train and equip or with the people in the streets? Would they rescue capital investments from the mob or defend the popular thirst for democracy? Or would America decide instead to do nothing, even though its policies of the past thirty years have been directly implicated in setting the stage for tragedy in Indonesia?

This is an extreme metaphor, to be sure, but it describes potential dilemmas that exist in many other countries and regions around the world. As globalizing production and finance undermine the command powers of the nation-state, the American military may find itself caught in the middle of many such questions. Is the military's purpose to defend the sovereign nation or the global economic system? Are the armed forces deployed in behalf of U.S.-based multinationals or U.S. citizens? Is the core objective to protect American values or the amorality of the marketplace?

Such stark choices did not arise during the Cold War, or if they did they were finessed. They remain unresolved. I do not suggest there are any simple answers, but America's drift into an ill-defined global stewardship invites a moment of reckoning on these deep questions of sovereignty, loyalty, and purpose. At present, the conflicts are not even acknowledged by authorities and experts, let alone debated in an open forum where citizens might consider the implications.

The United States cannot escape the gut question: What constitutes the national security interest in a world where superpower rivalry has disappeared but where globalizing commerce and finance steadily attack the old meanings of national sovereignty and interest?

My own optimistic view is that these new circumstances present us with an opening in history—an opportunity to reinvent international relationships and to reach, with distant societies, a higher plateau of shared goals. Americans have the capacity to help fashion that different future and lead others to see the potential. Our democratic values and generous spirit are fully resonant with progressive objectives for the world at large.

But first, Americans must say no to empire.

◄○►

What do Americans want, now that they have won the peace? To be left alone to enjoy it, many would answer. Certainly, most Americans do not want to go looking for trouble in the world. And, of course, many do still yearn for a simpler time in the past, when their vital young nation felt self-sufficient and believed it could turn its back on the entangling business of international politics. Those currents of opinion do exist, for sure, but they are negative responses to the question.

The startling news—startling because it gets scant recognition from the press and politicians—is that Americans also express an overwhelming consensus on some positive outlines for national security and global relations. These viewpoints are largely ignored by policy makers and political leaders, perhaps because the public's vision of the future is wildly at odds with the conventional wisdom of governing elites.

Here are some propositions that might be called the "People's Choices" for how to create a new world order, each proposal followed by the percentage of citizens who endorse it in a recent opinion survey:

The United States should use its position to get other countries to take action against world environmental problems.

93 PERCENT

There should be a general understanding among nations that any country threatening to use chemical or nuclear weapons must be stopped, even if that means the use of military force by the United States and other countries.

92 PERCENT

The United Nations should play a much bigger peacekeeping and diplomatic role than it did before the Gulf War.

86 PERCENT

The countries of the world should act together, not on their own, to deter and resist aggression.

85 PERCENT

The United Nations should tax international arms sales with the money going to famine relief and humanitarian aid.

83 PERCENT

The United States should use its position to promote democracy in Eastern Europe, the Middle East, and elsewhere in the world.

78 PERCENT

The use of force seldom solves problems. The United States and the United Nations should rely on economic sanctions, diplomatic pressure, and judicial remedies in handling international threats.

70 PERCENT

As this suggests, Americans as a whole are not hostile to the United Nations or other international venues for resolving conflict and maintaining peace. On the contrary, they greatly favor that approach to unilateral mobilizations by the United States. The same opinion survey asked them directly: "Thinking about the United States and the United Nations, when faced with future problems involving aggression, who should take the lead?" Across a series of polls, 80 to 85 percent chose the United Nations. Only 11 to 17 percent preferred that the United States take the lead.

Can this be the same American public we read about in the newspapers? The folks who supposedly despise the United Nations? Who are bored by foreign affairs, oblivious to global problems, ready to withdraw from the world? Evidently not.

Or perhaps there are two quite different "publics" present in American political life—one whose positive reflections are largely neglected and another whose fears or misgivings are endlessly massaged and amplified in order to energize political campaigns and causes. Certainly, the "progressive" public gets very little representation by political leaders of stature.

The standard political response to such forward-looking opinions as the ones I have cited is that these expressions are nothing more than wishful thinking—pious and uninformed sentiments that float disconnected from the real politics of governing. When asked about their goals, Americans do tend to opt for happy endings—good schools and full employment, universal health care, peace and prosperity. Why not? We are an optimistic, generous people.

172

But the positive aspirations of the American public do not count for much in politics, either on domestic matters or in foreign policy. That is one measure of the decayed condition of American democracy, one related to the absence of genuine dialogue and accountability between representatives and the represented. Knowing how easily poll results can be manipulated, smart politicians say: "Don't trust what the public believes it wants" (unless their yearnings can be packaged as rhetorical "issues" for campaigns). In any case, politicians have learned that they can safely ignore the public's idealistic goals without fear of retribution.

Put aside their cynicism for a moment and suppose that Americans really do mean what they say (and understand more about the world than cynics imagine). I would argue that these results are a more reliable reflection of the deeper public attitudes than the usual stream of narrow-gauge polling for current issues and campaigns. These findings are derived from a remarkable ten-year polling series called "Americans Talk Issues" (ATI) designed and sponsored by the financial entrepreneur Alan F. Kay.

Kay's surveys were different in that people were not forced into crude yes-or-no answers but given pro-and-con background material and then a broad range of opinions and options to consider, endorse, or reject. The ATI surveys went back to retest viewpoints regularly over a period of years, both before and after the end of the Cold War. The surveys found a striking consistency.

I would describe the overall outlook as cautiously internationalist: a majority of respondents believe that global responsibilities should be shared among many nations, are willing to support U.S. action against aggression if nothing else seems possible, but are also convinced that the international institutions and governing controls should be strengthened. In the aftermath of the Gulf War, people are not more eager for U.S. military adventures, but more convinced that keeping the peace should be handled by unified mechanisms among many nations.

A plurality sees globalization as a positive development, but the negative view increases over time, fed by downsizing and disappointments associated with the North American Free Trade Agreement (NAFTA). Majorities favor stronger global regulation of financial markets, labor rights, pollution, arms sales, and other matters. On some issues, an overwhelming consensus wants multigovernment rules and regulations.

Defense budgets should shrink, according to these respondents, and the cost burdens be shared more evenly with allied nations. Military foreign aid should be cut, along with the CIA and other intelligence agencies, nuclear warhead production and maintenance, and the space program. People like the idea of a global demilitarization fund (proposed by Costa Rica's Oscar Arias), which would help countries convert arms production to civilian uses.

The centerpiece of U.S. preparedness—the two-war strategy that justifies current defense spending—met with great skepticism. In an earlier survey, 68 percent said this premise for force planning is unnecessary because "we can count on the help of allies." Another group thought that getting ready for one regional war was plenty. Fewer still, less than 10 percent, endorsed the two-war assumptions. When the question was tested again in 1995 and people were told that "our leaders" in both political parties support the concept, many more people got on board. Still, only a bare majority of 51 percent was persuaded.

What all this indicates, at a minimum, is that American military leaders and foreign policy architects are marching in a different direction from the public's bolder vision of post–Cold War prospects. The lesson learned in Vietnam—that military interventions cannot be sustained without broad popular support—has lost much of its cautionary punch in governing circles, but it remains highly relevant to America's future.

Public opinion can be fickle, we know, and easily manipulated by propaganda blitzes in the form of clever TV commercials. But the broad, consistent aspirations expressed by the people should provide the basis for serious questioning of some of the specific policies the government is now pursuing in international affairs. Governing elites believe in their own expertise, but on some matters, unwashed public opinion is way ahead of the experts.

The government, for instance, actively promotes (and subsidizes) arms exports by U.S. manufacturers. The public thinks the global arms trade threatens peace. Indeed, people think all international arms sales, including U.S. weapons, should be taxed (not by Washington but by the United Nations). When opinion surveyors pointed out that taxes would dampen sales and may hurt American workers and companies, people did not back off.

Americans at large are preoccupied with the environmental crisis and put it at the very top of their list of global dangers. The administration did ultimately accept the Kyoto agreement on global warming, but not without first trying to use its muscle to water down the terms. And major industrial sectors are intent on blocking its implementation in Congress by sounding alarms about the supposedly dreadful economic impact for Americans.

It seems fair to ask: Who is doing the wishful thinking on this global environmental issue—the governing elites in politics and business or the untutored public?

In terms of economic self-interest, the American people may realize the job opportunities in the environmental problem even though their leaders do not yet recognize them. A study by Miriam Pemberton and Michael Renner of the National Commission on Economic Conversion and Disarmament notes that the world market for environmental technologies is double the global market for all types of military hardware. U.S. exports of enviro-tech goods already exceed arms exports, and the disparity is sure to widen.

Yet the U.S. government spends twelve times more on promoting arms sales abroad than on environmental technologies.

Japan, Germany, and other industrial nations that are not burdened by such an awesome defense industry are doing the opposite—and stealing the march on a growth sector that is more promising (and fruitful for the world) than weaponry.

America goes its own way on other global issues, despite the public yearning for greater cooperation. The international diplomacy that produced a new global treaty abolishing antipersonnel landmines was not led by Washington. The Pentagon objected. The White House acceded to the military's anxieties. Other nations persisted anyway (and rejected dilutions and exceptions demanded by the United States). In the end, the largest military establishment in the world—ours—stands outside the world consensus, joined by a few other outlier nations like China.

Likewise, the Clinton administration has blocked a new international treaty prohibiting the world's military forces from recruiting children under eighteen as armed troops. Washington also insists on limiting the powers of the new international criminal court that other nations seek to create. The ATI surveys found that Americans overwhelmingly support the creation of international judicial tribunals that will have the "force of law" to prevent and punish lawless behavior.

In sum, Washington assumes an influence over events that is fast eroding. If the present drift of events continues, the American government will find itself increasingly isolated from the world opinion it presumes to lead. It will also be alienated from its own people. This is not a formula for imperial stability.

◄○►

During the Cold War decades, revisionist historians delivered a most provocative critique of the permanent war mobilization: the imperial impulse is embedded in the American character. The national history, from colonial origins to "winning" the West, has followed an imperative of conquest and expansion, they argued, that led the country to evade the deep contradictions in a democracy that tolerates such great inequalities of wealth and power.

When the continental frontier was exhausted at the end of the nineteenth century, the nation turned abroad in search of new territories to acquire and dominate. After World War II, the Cold War kept alive these expansive energies, elaborated further by globalizing commerce and banking.

The logic and symmetry of the revisionist case was powerful, but I always rejected its dark, deterministic verdict on the American experience. It left out the spontaneous and generous, the playful and inventive qualities in the national character. It dismissed the yeoman tradition of individualism that seeks modest space and self-sufficiency, a yearning to control one's own destiny but not to meddle in other people's fights. The portrait of "empire as a way of life," as William Appleman Williams called it, seems to give up on democratic possibilities.

This question of national character is, nonetheless, before us again in the post–Cold War era. I continue to think that most

Americans do not wish to follow the road to empire, that they neither want nor require global domination for their pursuit of happiness. Still, I do concede that the revisionist case seems strengthened by current events, or at least by the neo-imperial aspirations of elites. Things are never put so starkly in politics or diplomacy, but the core question is about our values as a people. Do we wish to run the world or to create more mature arrangements among nations that can maintain peace and equity? Isn't the world ready for an end to empires, even ours?

An alternative vision of national security would accept that ever-expanding military obligations are not going to be in America's long-term interest. It sets up the nation as global cop, scurrying from one bonfire to another and hostage to the media's roving alarums, inevitably collecting resentment and enemies, inviting a moment of miscalculation when things go terribly wrong and America gets scapegoated as the arrogant bully.

Yet it is also true that the United States cannot easily escape from this role, given its awesome military power and capabilities, until convincing alternatives are constructed on an international scale. Since that challenge is so dauntingly difficult and many others are happy to let America do the nasty heavy lifting, the present drift continues toward a moment someday of surprise and humiliation. This is unlikely to change much until American political leaders find the courage to confront these big questions and begin describing a genuinely different framework for national—that is, global—security.

To put this more concretely, the United States would have to commit its power to constructing international security forces and mechanisms for conflict resolution that everyone can trust. Instead of standing aloof, pretending that U.S. influence is undiminished by the end of the superpower rivalry, America would have to devote its diplomatic power (and sense of invention) to creating new institutions and strengthening old ones like the United Nations.

This does not require "world government" or a "UN army," but it would certainly reverse many present U.S. defense policies, including the reliance on arms exports to prop up the underutilized defense factories. If this sounds utopian, it is actually updated realism—a new geopolitics that understands the dangers of continuing the arms proliferation. The United States is the major seller now, even as it scolds other nations equipping themselves for self-defense or for aggression.

The rest of the world is not blind. It can see America planning and producing spectacular new weapons systems when its arsenal is already overwhelmingly superior and deeply redundant. Other nations, large and small, ask themselves: What do those Americans have in mind for their new super-weapons? Is it self-defense or dominion?

If I am correct that global economic forces are sowing potential conflicts more certainly than balance-of-power issues about armaments, then reforming the global economic system is central to national security. The present unfolding crisis presents the opportunity for large reforms and makes the need clear.

The United States should be leading the debate and diplomacy toward formation of a new Bretton Woods agreement that restores stability and equity among both rich and poor, for the developing nations as well as for established industrial powers. Among other things, this would require imposing moderating controls on capital flows, a new system to anchor currency values, and the serious introduction of human rights and other social values into the terms of trade. That is, governments will have to reassert responsibility. The illusion that unregulated markets lead to stability and equity has been smashed, again and again, by recurring crisis and upheaval.

Like global security arrangements, the global economic system has to work for everyone if it is to endure. So the work of devising reforms cannot be left to economists and bankers, nor can it be dictated by the major industrial powers. Global politics involves bringing everyone to the table, labor and capital, producers and environmentalists, the rich nations and the struggling poor. If Washington decided to lead forcefully on this initiative, it would have to turn on some of its political patrons, but it might be surprised to find many new allies around the world eager to enlist with their ideas.

Where would all this leave the military-industrial complex?

Obviously, a lot smaller. Genuine sharing of military burdens means reducing the size of both U.S. armed forces and the defense industrial base. Many military leaders already accept that prospect as inevitable (at least among themselves) and have various concepts for how to shrink the force structure sensibly and substantially. One cannot say the same for surviving behemoths in the defense industry.

Settling for less of the same is not a solution.

To recapitulate my argument, the military-industrial complex is stuck in an untenable condition. The armed services, trying to sustain their old structure and acquire new weaponry and reform war-making for the future, are compelled to steadily degrade and devour their own capabilities. Whatever happens next in the world, the U.S. defense remains matched against the past.

The short, painful message is this: the armed forces ought to be both realigned in purpose and greatly reduced in size. I do not claim the expertise to be able to describe the correct size and design of the force structure, but as I've illustrated, there are already plenty of smart proposals from sophisticated planners on how to shrink the uniformed services and achieve greater effectiveness. Those military thinkers all recognize the same point I have made: if fundamental change doesn't occur, the vast arsenal will become increasingly incoherent and hollow—mismatched against the new global realities.

The armaments industry, meanwhile, is even more irrational in its inherited structure. Still grossly too large, it keeps the factories alive at taxpayer expense, waiting for the next boom to come along, just as it has done for decades since World War II.

Isn't it time we got over the specter of Pearl Harbor? Given our awesome technological advantages, what are we so afraid of? The flexible inventiveness of American enterprise is a far greater asset for national defense than hanging on to idle factories that were built half a century ago to fight Japan and Germany.

There is a hidden cost to not demobilizing, of continuing to finance an oversized defense industrial base that remains poised for another war, another arms buildup. This cost is the tangible threat to global peace. One consequence of keeping the old factories in place is the inevitable business imperative to sell our advanced arms to the rest of the world, while we build better ones for ourselves. Devoting government subsidies to this also neglects the competing national priorities and promising sectors for alternative products that could use government help. Promoting weapons as a prime American export keeps the defense factories warm, but it will someday come back to haunt us, somewhere in the world. At present, we are indulging the industrial past.

In a sense, my argument for a fundamental reordering of global priorities takes some of the heat off the Pentagon and the armed forces. The people in uniform cannot be blamed for the political vacuum. Nor is it realistic to expect them to dismantle their institutions unilaterally in the absence of strong political direction. The armed services, like other sectors, are only beginning to grasp the security implications of the global economic system that puts them in the middle. They cannot settle those economic issues, obviously, but they ought to start challenging the fuzzy assumptions about how military power is supposed to be used for economic conflict.

In the end, the dilemmas facing Fortress America are political. Given the weak hold that both political parties have on a voting majority, neither has the nerve to take on the challenges I have been describing. These ideas sound risky, or somehow weak, alongside the usual politics of maintaining America's overwhelming military might. Smart politics tries instead to finesse the big questions, cutting and squeezing a little bit here and there, changing as little as possible.

Still, I think the American people are ready to hear something different. They are more open to dramatic changes in national defense than status-quo Washington imagines. They await a real debate. Politicians who describe the new global realities honestly and offer plausible, forward-looking responses will find themselves becoming the party of the future.

AFTERWORD

The short war for Kosovo in the spring of 1999 was distinctive in its methodology and enervating in the aftermath. While President Clinton declared a victory for humanitarian values, there was not the "bounce" in his public-opinion approval ratings that a commander-in-chief usually enjoys after military action. No one called this a "splendid little war" or suggested it provides a model for the future of international peacekeeping. Messy contradictions muted any sense of celebration.

The brutal ethnic cleansing conducted by Slobodan Milosevic and the Serbians was halted in the province and refugees returned home, though it was possible to argue that NATO's air attacks gave cover for the sweep of massacres and displacements that occurred. In any case, the murder, arson and random savagery did not stop in Kosovo. The cleansing was taken up by vengeful Albanians, eager to rid their villages and cities of the Serbian minority. Neither NATO's occupying forces of 50,000 troops nor United Nations peace supervisors seemed able to halt this bloodletting, either by persuasion or by force of arms. The peacekeepers dispatched fire trucks to burning houses, while troops protected the firefighters from Albanian snipers. The people who had just been rescued from oppression were now shooting at the forces who rescued them.

Like Saddam Hussein before him, Milosevic remained in power, though beleaguered by popular opposition. The nation of Serbia was devastated. The country's economic infrastructure would not be rebuilt, the allies warned, until it changed its government.

This outcome, despite the many ambiguities, was described by some as a victory for air power. About 14,000 bombs and missiles were expended against Serbia (though a handful of the guided missiles actually landed in Bulgaria). A variety of modern military aircraft participated and flew more than 12,000 strike sorties, according to a compilation by *The Wall Street Journal.* Most of the allied planes were American (720 out of 1,068). The U.S. Air Force even managed to deploy its controversial new bombers—the B-1 and B-2—in real combat for the first time. The energies of a real war, of course, create demand for weapons production. Raytheon expected $1 billion in cruise-missile orders to replenish the arsenal. Air Force enthusiasts began arguing for development of another new bomber, one that would be even stealthier than the B-2.

The Pentagon emphasized the Serbian military targets it had destroyed—120 tanks, 314 artillery pieces, more than 100 aircraft, fourteen command posts. But anyone could see for themselves on television that spectacular raids were also conducted against Serbian cities, factories and refineries, bridges across the Danube and also, with the usual chaos of war, against trains, buses, and hospitals.

The U.S. Army, meanwhile, did not participate in this war, despite its thousands of highly capable tanks and attack helicopters. To deploy ground troops, as leaders understood, would likely produce casualties. Instead, the Army was sent in afterwards as a constabulatory force to police the troubled peace.

The allied forces lost three people (two Americans killed in the crash of an Apache helicopter and one German who died in a tank accident). The Serbs suffered at least 15,000 military casualties, killed or wounded, according to NATO. Another 6,500 civilians were killed or injured by NATO bombs, according to the Yugoslav government. Thousands more died at the hands of the Serbian paramilitary thugs. None of these preliminary casualty estimates was especially reliable, but the numbers demonstrate the one-sided nature of the conflict.

Industrialized warfare in this age of high-technology weaponry creates a bizarre opportunity—the casualty-free war. A nation with the right equipment might plan and execute a campaign of mass destruction with high confidence that it will suffer very few losses itself—assuming it chooses only adversaries who are too small or poor to possess the same advanced weaponry. This overwhelming advantage in destructive power allows—perhaps even encourages—a nation to use military force for quite limited diplomatic objectives, compelling another sovereign government to change its policy and politics. A punitive aggression is launched, not to conquer and hold territory, but to deliver diplomatic ultimatums. "Sign the peace agreement or we will bomb you." "Accept our terms or we will escalate the destruction." "Give in, resign or we will destroy the economic life of your society."

Karl von Clausewitz's famous dictum—war as the logical extension of diplomacy—is stood on its head. Now the diplomacy waits upon the war. The negotiations will be settled, not necessarily by just objectives or international law or patient mediation among competing grievances. The terms will be decided, ultimately, by thousands of airborne explosives delivered from a great distance. If necessary, many of the bombs and missiles will be directed at the civilian population (albeit with a flimsy rationale that the targets involve vital military resources). The battlefield, once defined as armies meeting on a field of violent conflict, dissolves into an amorphous realm of conflict—public opinion. How long will the war last? Until the people can no longer stand it, until they rise up and throw out their government.

Does this sound like a promising path toward maintaining world order? I think it is more likely that we—the United States especially—have unwittingly crossed a dangerous threshold. What I am trying to suggest is that ancient barbarism lurks at the center of these new circumstances for pristine war-making. It is not necessary to blink away the crimes of the Serbian government in order to see the problem. A nation willing to visit long-range destruction upon other societies—without observing any of the traditional checkpoints for launching an aggression—has perhaps entered its own patch of moral quicksand.

The United States, in particular, has cast itself as a kind of "good guy" empire that will selectively enforce good order and humane behavior around the world. It claims prerogatives of power for itself that are beyond review by others and beyond the established standards of international law. The ability to use destructive force unilaterally—that is, with no real danger of retaliation from the enemy—resembles the temptation of original sin. Once modern societies learn they can indulge their lopsided technological advantage in this manner—fight the casualty-free war without consequences—it may be very hard for political leaders to foreswear the practice or, for that matter, to propose engaging in a real war that promises real human losses in return. Why must any Americans die at all? Can't we just bomb those other people into oblivion?

This is new ground in the story of war, I think, though it might eventually resemble the purposeful siege and slaughter tactics employed in medieval times and before. The earnest efforts of internationalists to construct civilized rules that prohibit or at least contain the massive killing of twentieth-century warfare are undone by wondrous inventions. Why surround a city with a siege army and starve its inhabitants into submission when one can send scores of cruise missiles from hundreds of miles away?

The messy aftermath of Kosovo, I concede, does not suggest that any government, including America's, will be eager anytime soon to repeat this episode, not without great provocation. But this practice of unilateral attack on other nations—countries not previously identified as an aggressor or posing any obvious threat to U.S. security—did not start with Kosovo nor did it likely end there. If the practice comes into routine acceptance as legitimate, Americans will have lost constitutional protections against their government's abuse of power. And the world at large will be confronted with dangerous new power relationships, in which the strong feel free to subjugate the weak in the name of high-minded purposes.

To make the point more precisely, the NATO alliance attacked a nation that was not at war with any of its members nor threatening to make war. The justification was Serbia's gross humanitarian crimes against its own citizens, but it was also true that Serbia faced civil war—an armed insurgency that demanded sovereign independence for Kosovar Albanians and conducted its own terror campaign against Serbian citizens and government officials. What principle was established by this engagement—that the U.S. or others may intervene elsewhere when a government is employing abusive methods to suppress a civil rebellion?

If so, there are many opportunities for intervention, from the Mexican army's campaign against the oppressed ethnic minority in Chiapas to Indonesia's long, brutal war against the once-independent people of East Timor. I do not suggest that the U.S. would respond in those cases or others. Indeed, the U.S. passed on intervening in Rwanda, clearly the greatest case of genocide in this decade where half a million people were slaughtered and a modest, military expedition might have stopped the killing. My point is: There is no overarching principle at stake, not one that any powerful nation seriously intends to uphold.

The United States, in fact, has once again ignored its own lawful standards for war-making, that is, the Constitution. The business of engaging in foreign military action without bothering to declare war has become so commonplace in the modern era that it now seems quaint to raise the objection. In most instances during the Cold War, however, presidents could at least claim a threatening emergency and argue that the nation's defense required an immediate executive response. In this new era, the incidents are defining a new category of principled war-making in which national security is not even at issue, though the military action may make Americans feel virtuous about their role in the world.

A "humanitarian war" is a ghastly contradiction in terms, as the experience in Kosovo made plain. As every soldier understands, war is organized violence and the high precision of modern weaponry does not eliminate bloody accidents and misguided missiles. The same public that was horrified by Milosevic's methods was anguished at the sight of innocent children killed or maimed by American bombs. The Chinese were understandably skeptical that the awesome technological prowess of the United States had somehow bombed their embassy in Belgrade by mistake.

What is less obvious to Americans is that the policy of pursuing casualty-free war undoubtedly worsens the destruction of innocents on the other side—and very likely violates the same international covenants on humane conduct that the U.S. was presumably trying to uphold. Most of the massive bombing campaign in Serbia was conducted at high altitudes in order to lessen the possibility that allied aircraft would be shot down. Inevitably, that increases inaccuracy and the likelihood that some bombs hit unintended targets.

"The decision to minimize risk to American soldiers [by bombing only from high altitudes, for example] becomes morally problematic if that either increases the substantive risks for civilians—bombs dropped randomly—or it reduces the prospect of a successful end to the killing," Kenneth Roth, executive director of Human Rights Watch, asserted.

Did the NATO forces themselves violate the Geneva conventions by actively targeting civilian populations? The military authorities insist not, but the evidence is suspicious. Human Rights Watch was prompted to demand a formal investigation into whether the allied strategy committed a "grave breach of humanitarian law." The rules of war adopted by nations after World War II attempt to establish a bright line between military targets and punishing civilians for political reasons. The fact that NATO bombed electrical transformers in cities, TV and radio transmission towers, even a tobacco factory and warehouse owned by key supporters of Milosevic, suggests the real purpose was to demoralize civilians or silence propaganda broadcasts or darken residential neighborhoods, Roth observed.

Furthermore, the heavy use of cluster bombs may have violated the new international agreement prohibiting the use of landmines since these devices scatter dozens of small bomblets, many of which do not explode and fall to the ground as potential landmines. These are especially dangerous for children who are attracted to the bright orange-yellow objects that resemble a soda pop can or baseball. In April, five children were killed and two injured near Doganovic in southern Kosovo while playing with these unexploded bombs. After the war, several French peacekeeping soldiers were killed in the same manner. "Like any anti-personnel landmines, cluster bombs kill civilians even years after the conflict has ended," said Joost R. Hiltermann, director of the Arms Project at Human Rights Watch. NATO ignored the group's plea to stop using these weapons. Perhaps cluster bombs have something to do with why the U.S. refused to sign the new landmine treaty, though other NATO nations did.

All of these complaints may sound a bit precious alongside the enormity of Milosevic's brutalities. The Serbian leader, we were told, is the Hitler of our time and must be stopped at any cost. But this propaganda is unpersuasive and raises more questions about the principle at stake. If Milosevic is Hitler, then

193

why were the NATO nations shadow-boxing with him, promising not to send in an invading army to conquer and capture him as a war criminal? Why, for that matter, is Milosevic still allowed to govern Serbia, while an occupying army of Americans and Europeans patrols the villages of Kosovo just down the road? The answer is the same. Even if Milosevic represented evil on the scale of Hitler, the U.S. was unwilling to risk American casualties in order to remove him.

Kenneth Roth is not alone in suspecting that the real motivation for the Kosovo intervention was preserving the credibility of NATO or a dubious domino-theory scenario for the Balkans. The United States, by asserting its singular power to decide these matters while scorning the efforts to create new international agreements on war and weaponry, may actually be blocking the road to a more stable, more humane world.

American leaders stand aloof from the new treaties on landmines and an international criminal court, Roth noted, because "they say we have special duties and therefore we deserve special exceptions. It's an argument of American exceptionalism. The problem with that, of course, is that it's not a system of justice when you exempt the big guy from law."

In many ways, these unanswered questions about how America intends to use its military power are more crucial than the budget issues about what kind of weaponry and armed forces are needed. In any case, until the American public confronts the new moral implications of our firepower, it is not likely to think clearly about how much is too much.

—◦—

The weapons industry has lost its glow since *Fortress America* was first published, with corporate profits and stock prices declining sharply. On the other hand, the companies may now be convinced that their painful lull in defense spending is finally ending. Both Republicans and Democrats are promising to reverse the post-Cold War trend and begin appropriating major budget increases for the Pentagon again, especially for procurement. The public seems to be slowly awakening to the implications. With luck, we may witness a genuine argument over national priorities during the presidential campaign in 2000 but, if so, it must be generated by alarmed citizens since honest debate and reform isn't likely to emerge from Washington.

The military-industrial complex's collision between desire and wherewithal has ripened considerably in the last few years—that is, the gap between available funding and spending commitments has steadily widened. This was no secret to insiders, of course, but it took a very public turn in the fall of 1998 when the Joint Chiefs of Staff reluctantly acknowledged to the Senate armed services committee that, yes, the internal budget tensions are beginning to have a deteriorating impact on the fighting readiness of the forces. Many senators who knew better professed to be shocked.

In the political theater that followed, Senator McCain asked the service chiefs to enumerate exactly what it would take to bring the U.S. armed forces up to speed. Their collective answer was a bountiful wish list, totaling $125 billion. Both parties expressed a desire to increase the Pentagon's budget in real terms (especially if the money was improving conditions for servicemen and women) and began to do so modestly, with an $8 billion add-on in 1998. In his next budget, President Clinton proposed much more: cumulative increases that would eventually take the defense budget to around $310 billion. Republicans naturally topped that and embraced a goal of defense spending around $350 billion.

The prospect is breathtaking—the nation expanding its military budget by nearly one third in the midst of general peace. Fortunately, that prospect is also quite fictional, though the election-season rhetoric makes it especially difficult to know what the real intentions are. The more expansive numbers are impossible to achieve, in any case. First, there are the competing priorities under the rigorous budget ceilings imposed since 1997. Even with supposed surpluses ahead for the federal government, Congress cannot break the spending caps on defense without taking the money from somewhere else.

As this reality unfolds during the next few years, the contest may finally form around questions of priority: Shall we fund Medicare and Medicaid or build more attack submarines? Do we need those aircraft carriers more than we need new schools or more teachers? That at least is the hopeful possibility. A new organization—Business Leaders for Sensible Priorities—has been launched by progressive executives and former military leaders to sharpen the debate in exactly this way. Led by Ben Cohen, co-founder of Ben & Jerry's Ice Cream, the group intends to conduct a broad campaign of public education, along with many pointed questions directed at the candidates.

The goal of Business Leaders for Sensible Priorities is modest and rational. Based on budget analysis by respected military experts, the group argues that, instead of increases, the defense budget should be reduced by $40 billion a year and the money shifted to domestic needs. This can be accomplished without injury to national security, as many military authorities know and have written themselves. The question really is: how long will the political nostalgia for the Cold War allow the military to ride along free—without serious reform—while expending tens of billions on yesterday's defense system? The day of reckoning seems closer.

Hard choices, in other words, are sure to get harder for the Pentagon, even if it does win modest budget increases. That reality was reflected in the summer of 1999 when the House appropriators abruptly tried to kill financing for the F-22 production. The Air Force and Lockheed Martin would fight back, of course, but the action revealed that even hawkish Republicans are desperate for solutions to the underlying dilemma. Even with budget increases, even if the F-22 is cancelled, the military-industrial complex will still not be able to pay for everything it has ordered up. So the weaker projects become more vulnerable, even as the arms companies dream up grandiose new schemes for a safer America.

The ideal remedy, of course, is what this book argues for: a genuine, robust re-examination of national defense in this new world without a major enemy, a hard-nosed scrutiny of the perpetual technical additions to existing weaponry, a smart but sympathetic restructuring of the uniformed forces themselves. If we cannot have such a patient and rational discussion, then let us hope for the next best thing: that the American people will eventually, finally, get angry—angry about the wasted billions and misplaced national priorities—and take their anger out on the elected politicians who neglect these great questions. If such vengeance is someday visited on the politicians and the military and the weapons makers, they will have earned it.

‹o›

ACKNOWLEDGMENTS

Jann S. Wenner, editor of *Rolling Stone,* should get full esteem (or blame in some quarters) for the parentage of this book. I have been writing for Jann for more than fifteen years. We share the same optimistic political values and a resilient conviction that our country has not yet reached its best potential, but that it can, and someday will, if people will speak to the possibilities.

In that spirit, we converged on the same insight about the defense establishment: long after the fall of the Soviet Union, the Cold War status quo was enduring essentially unaltered, its contradictions largely evaded by national politics. The examination that followed involved a lot of digging and traveling and produced the three-part series in *Rolling Stone* that provides the basis for this book. I have expanded the text and scope in various ways, but it was Jann Wenner who nudged me to expand my own vision of the subject.

I thank him for his boldness, and I thank the staff of *Rolling Stone.* Can you think of another mass-circulation, popular magazine that would commit the space and resources for such an inquiry? I can't.

Secondly, I am proud to be on the very first season's list to be published by Peter Osnos at PublicAffairs. Peter is an old friend, too, my partner in managing the national staff at the *Washington Post* nearly twenty years ago. This new house is based on his marketing insights about how to publish valuable books on public affairs, politics, history, and other serious matters, and do so profitably. I thank him, editor Geoff Shandler, and the staff.

Finally, I wish to recognize another old friend and former associate, George Wilson, who provided far-sighted tutoring for this project. George's own reporting is legendary in military circles. (I interviewed one young Army officer who referred to him as "Colonel Wilson," though George served as an enlisted man, as did I.) For three decades, he was the astute Pentagon reporter at the *Post,* and he has since written a series of wonderful books about the bone and sinew of the military, the people, from grunts to generals. I've long relied on him as my personal guru on defense matters. I thank him again for his generous guidance.

PublicAffairs is a new nonfiction publishing house and a tribute to the standards, values, and flair of three persons who have served as mentors to countless reporters, writers, editors, and book people of all kinds, including me.

I. F. Stone, proprietor of *I. F. Stone's Weekly*, combined a commitment to the First Amendment with entrepreneurial zeal and reporting skill and became one of the great independent journalists in American history. At the age of eighty, Izzy published *The Trial of Socrates*, which was a national bestseller. He wrote the book after he taught himself ancient Greek.

Benjamin C. Bradlee was for nearly thirty years the charismatic editorial leader of *The Washington Post*. It was Ben who gave the *Post* the range and courage to pursue such historic issues as Watergate. He supported his reporters with a tenacity that made them fearless, and it is no accident that so many became authors of influential, bestselling books.

Robert L. Bernstein, the chief executive of Random House for more than a quarter century, guided one of the nation's premier publishing houses. Bob was personally responsible for many books of political dissent and argument that challenged tyranny around the globe. He is also the founder and was the longtime chair of Human Rights Watch, one of the most respected human rights organizations in the world.

◄o►

For fifty years, the banner of Public Affairs Press was carried by its owner, Morris B. Schnapper, who published Gandhi, Nasser, Toynbee, Truman, and about 1,500 other authors. In 1983 Schnapper was described by *The Washington Post* as "a redoubtable gadfly." His legacy will endure in the books to come.

Peter Osnos, *Publisher*